Praise for *Mastering the Complex Sale*

"Jeff's approach to creating and keeping win-win customer relationships has been nothing short of life transforming. Today we only invest in companies that agree to adopt the Prime philosophy and process."

—Richard Koffler, CEO, Koffler Ventures LLC

"Thull's insight into 'business think' vs. 'sales think' will bring you exceptional credibility. *Mastering the Complex Sale* is a must-read for today's competitive landscape in the financial services arena."

—Jeff Nicholson, Managing Director &
Market Executive, Harris Nesbitt

"We've ingrained the Prime Process in our culture around the globe and it's clearly a sustainable competitive advantage. I write this endorsement with some reluctance as I don't want my competitors to have this advantage. In 30 years of reading books and attending seminars to continue my professional growth, there are only a handful that I can say made a difference. Jeff Thull's *Mastering the Complex Sale* is one of them."

—Jim Clouser, President and COO,
IBA Technology Group—Belgium

"We have found the Prime Process invaluable. It provides a blueprint superior to all other methodologies we have tried. We particularly like the high integrity approach. *Mastering the Complex Sale* is a must-read for everyone selling capital equipment or supporting someone who does."

—Ken Anderson, Senior Vice President, Instron

"Jeff's approach to the complex sale is both accurate and insightful, and for any sales organization that embraces and puts *Mastering the Complex Sale* into practice, the models and strategies of the Prime Process will bring them a tremendous business advantage."

—Stan Luboda, Vice President, Americas, Cognex

"Approaching the complex sale as a decision process, not a sales process, takes customer focus, win-win, and mutual respect to a new level. The Prime Process is clearly the way to do business."

—Robert Priest-Heck, COO, Key3 Media Events,
producers of COMDEX NetWorld+Interop

"If you're tired of being the 'unpaid consultant' and engaging in countless 'dry runs,' Thull's *Mastering the Complex Sale* shows you how to cut through the clutter and cut to the chase. This book gives you everything you need for transition from conventional to complex sales. A real adventure!"

—Per Lofving, Group Vice President, Thomas Publishing

"Jeff Thull presents a philosophical approach to the sales process required to master high-dollar complex sales situations that is unlike any other that I have seen."

—Bob Brockman, Chairman and CEO, Universal Computer Systems, Inc.

"*Mastering the Complex Sale* is the most enlightened approach you will find to address the complexities of today's business world, clearly a balanced approach to business and personal success."

—Tom Gegax, Author, Winning in the Game of Life, Co-Founder Tires Plus, CEO, Gegax Consulting and Keynotes

"*Mastering the Complex Sale* will open your eyes to the ways of today's market, giving you a new perspective of the sales cycle and the opportunities available to those willing to embrace change."

—David J. Fasbender, Sr. Vice President—Sales & Marketing, Smead Manufacturing Co.

"Jeff Thull has done a brilliant job of capturing a straightforward and immensely lucrative way for you to get a handle on complex sales. He takes you to the heart of creating measurable value for your customers, resulting in increased margins and customer loyalty."

—Charles W. Morris, V. P. Specialty Chemicals and Resins, Georgia-Pacific

"A roadmap for graduating from messenger of information to mentor of customers, *Mastering the Complex Sale* will be devoured by sales professionals—people who seek not only career success but personal fulfillment from their high calling."

—Carl T. Holst-Knudsen, President, Thomas Publishing

"In today's tough technology climate the stakes are high for every opportunity. *Mastering the Complex Sale* is a blueprint for understanding how to increase your customers' awareness of their business issues by managing the decision process, a winning formula that should be utilized on every sales call. It's not only thought provoking but right on the mark. This is the future of high-stakes selling."

—Michael W. Liacko, Sr. Vice President Corporate Sales, Key3 Media Events

Mastering the Complex Sale

HOW TO COMPETE AND WIN WHEN THE STAKES ARE HIGH!

JEFF THULL

WILEY

JOHN WILEY & SONS, INC.

Published by John Wiley & Sons, Inc., Hoboken, New Jersey.
Published simultaneously in Canada.

For general information on our other products and services please contact our Customer Care Department within the United States at (800) 762-2974, outside the United States at (317) 572-3993 or fax (317) 572-4002.

Wiley also publishes its books in a variety of electronic formats. Some content that appears in print may not be available in electronic books. For more information about Wiley products, visit our Web site at www.wiley.com.

Mastering the Complex Sale®, Diagnostic Selling®, Diagnostic Business Development®, and Prime Resource Group®, are registered trademarks of Prime Resource Group, Inc. Diagnostic Marketing™, Diagnostic Map™, Mastering Executive Relationships™, Key Thoughts™, and Multiple Decisions/Mutual Understandings™, are trademarks of Prime Resource Group, Inc.

For more information about Prime Resource Group, visit our Web site at www.primeresource.com or contact Customer Support within the U.S. at (800) 876-0378, outside the United States at (763) 473-7529 or e-mail support@primeresource.com.

Library of Congress Cataloging-in-Publication Data:

Thull, Jeff, 1949–
   Mastering the complex sale : how to compete and win when the stakes
are high! / Jeff Thull.
     p. cm.
   Includes bibliographical references and index.
   ISBN 0-471-43151-6 (cloth : paper)
   1. Selling—Handbooks, manuals, etc. 2. Relationship
marketing—Handbooks, manuals, etc. I. Title.
   HF5438.25.T525   2003
   658.85—dc21

                                      2002153141

Printed in the United States of America.

10 9 8 7 6 5

Foreword

Are your sales strategies, processes, and skills stuck in the wrong era?

The businesses we sell to, the problems we solve, and the solutions we offer have evolved tremendously in the past 50 years. This raises a few questions: "Can you, as a salesperson, a manager, or an organization, effectively compete in today's market?" The fact is, a high percentage of salespeople and the organizations they work for haven't kept pace with this evolution.

We're living and working in a time I've come to refer to as "the third era of selling." Understanding the history of this evolution is an important factor to moving forward into Era 3. So let me step back with you for a moment.

Several years ago, I was asked to teach a course in Instructional Design, at the University of Minnesota, as it relates to "Sales Training." As the instructor, you are obliged—in any introductory course—to work a short "History of This Discipline" speech into the first class session. As I surveyed what literature there was on the subject, I found that sales, unlike most other functions in the modern corporation, didn't really have much of a "history." At least, nobody studied and wrote about selling in the same way that they studied and wrote about Marketing, Logistics, Quality, Operations, or General Management. Even Purchasing has a longer academic pedigree than Sales.

I figured that the best way to find a window on the history of selling was to look at the evolution of sales training. I would study the skills salespeople were taught to find clues about what their role was seen to be. Feeling like an archeologist, I went to a couple of libraries and checked out all the material I could find that addressed the question, "How can I be more successful in sales?" It turned out to be quite a load of stuff: training manuals, articles, recordings (LP records from the 50s, up through cassettes and CDs of today), brochures, and lots of books. I was surprised to find that they all sorted into three main piles, piles representing what I've come to call Era 1, Era 2, and Era 3 of selling.

Era 1

The earliest material in the Era 1 pile dated from the early 1950s. A reviewer today would characterize the titles of some of the books in that pile as somewhere between naïve and appalling: *The Customer Who Can't Say No!*, *Sizzlemanship!!*, and the ever-popular, *1001 Power Closes!!!* But the skills just under the surface were both subtle and sophisticated. This was the era of the sales script ("Just tell me where to go and what to say when I get there."). The agenda was purely the seller's agenda, and the seller's agenda was to get the customer to do what he (and in some few cases, she) wanted the customer to do. The role of the Era 1 salesperson was that of *persuader*. The training focused almost exclusively on three areas: presenting, handling objections, and of course, closing. The skills were grounded in stimulus-response and compliance theories. Look at closing techniques, for example. If you strip away the exclamation marks, Era 1 techniques are based on the proven psychology of scaled commitments, reciprocation, compliant behavior of similar others, cues of legitimate authority, and cues of scarcity and friendship.

Era 1 still thrives in a few niches today (telemarketing and the used-car lot come to mind), but as an approach it has thankfully run out of gas. Why? Basically, customers caught onto the Win/Lose scam and developed defense mechanisms that salespeople even today (regardless of their orientation) have to cope with. Era 1 was replaced by an emphasis on a new set of skills, and by a new—and more enlightened—point of view about the role of the salesperson.

Era 2

The Era 2 alternative started emerging in the early and middle 1970s, with Larry Wilson and his "Counselor Approach" and Mac Hanan with his "Consultative Approach" being two of the earliest proponents. The emphasis on presenting, closing, and handling objections characteristic of Era 1 is replaced in Era 2 with a focus on questioning, listening, trust, and building a relationship with the customer. You won't find any reference to listening in any Era 1 material—because listening had absolutely no relevance to the Era 1 job. The questioning techniques of Era 2 were aimed at developing an understanding of the customer's needs (defined as the difference between what the customer has and what the customer wants), and the job of the salesperson was to understand and then close that gap with his or her product, the "solution." The Era 2 approach has come to be known as "needs-satisfaction selling," and the role of the Era 2 salesperson is that of *problem solver*.

Because it was grounded in a Win/Win rather than a Win/Lose point of view, Era 2 has enjoyed a longer run than Era 1 did. In fact, Era 2 remains the basis for much of the training that salespeople experience even today. But as the marketplace advanced, Era 2 needed to be supplemented (rather than replaced) for two reasons:

1. At the business level of the complex sale, most everybody is using an Era 2 to some degree. Early in Era 2, when most salespeople were still using Era 1

techniques, a salesperson could create differentiation—and get the business—simply by taking the needs-satisfaction approach. As more and more salespeople thought of questioning, listening, and solving customer problems as part of their job, the approach itself no longer provided any differentiation.

2. Customers, for the most part, aren't as experienced as they need to be. Needs-satisfaction selling is based on the assumption that the customer can accurately identify and describe their problem. Whether this assumption was ever really valid is open to debate. But as the complexity of business problems and the technology of solutions have developed over the past ten or so years, it's clearly questionable today.

So Era 2 skills continue to be necessary; they're just no longer sufficient.

Era 3

Era 3 took shape more slowly than Era 2 did, and it represents a convergence of two main influences, both of which could be described under the general rubric of "business acumen." If the role of the salesperson in Era 1 was that of a *persuader*, and in Era 2, that of a *problem solver*, the emerging role of the salesperson in Era 3 could be described as being a business person, specifically a *source of business advantage*. The thought of sales as a source of advantage is a pretty radical notion. Traditionally, the sales function is viewed by the rest of the organization as a kind of placement officer for the warehouse. Marketing is the brains, and Sales is the mouth and the feet.

As a source of advantage, the Era 3 salesperson is challenged to think from very different and complementary perspectives, both at the same time. One point of view is that of the "consultant," being a source of business advantage to the customer. When operating from this point of view, the salesperson must think like a business person and apply his or her business acumen and understanding of the customer's business processes and priorities to creating a solution that (to paraphrase Peter Senge) the customer would truly value, but has never experienced and would never think to ask for. Clearly beyond needs-satisfaction selling.

The other point of view is that of the "strategist"—the flipside of business acumen. He or she must think like a business person, from the point of view of their own company. In Era 1 and Era 2, the salesperson was concerned only with revenue. Margins and cost of sales were somebody else's problem. That paradigm never did work very well, even in the 1990s. Today, it's a formula for Chapter 11. So Era 3 salespeople are concerned not just with revenues, but also with cost of sales: shortening the sales cycle, ruthlessly qualifying opportunities, and walking away from unprofitable business. In short, as a "business person/ consultant," Era 3 salespeople are sources of advantage to their customers, while as a "business person/strategist," they are a source of advantage to their own firm. Two perspectives, one head, same time.

The Eras and Mastering the Complex Sale

At this point, you may be asking yourself what, if anything, this excursion down the Memory Lane of sales has to do with Jeff Thull and *Mastering the Complex Sale*. When I first met Jeff, upwards of five years ago, I thought I'd seen pretty much everything to be seen on the subject of selling. The more I've gotten to know and work with Jeff and Prime Resource Group, the more I realize how wrong I was.

The key challenge for the customer in Era 3 is two fold: First of all, the customer frequently does not have the high quality decision processes required to understand the complex problems they are experiencing. They also lack the extension of that decision process to understand the uniqueness of the complex solutions available to address those problems. Secondly, they require guidance and support in managing the organizational changes that are required to implement today's complex business solutions. To be a true source of business advantage, Era 3 sales professionals must address both of these challenges and the Prime Process provides an integrated approach that will do just that.

Jeff's philosophy of sales and the process he has developed, represent a genuinely and uniquely Era 3 point of view. I describe Jeff's approach as *genuinely* Era 3 in that the process, while totally respectful of the customer, doesn't assume that the customer has the complete picture or all the answers. The process is one of mutual engagement, understanding the scope and cost of the issues, and jointly creating a solution. The job of the salesperson is to manage the customer's decision process towards a decision that represents the best outcome for both parties.

His approach is *uniquely* Era 3 in that it encompasses both Era 3 roles or perspectives at once. You can point to other programs that focus exclusively on the "strategist" side of Era 3, and others that focus exclusively on the "consultant" side. Jeff's is the only approach that represents both at the same time: "No unpaid consulting," "Going for the no," and "Always be leaving" (the strategist), and "The Decision Challenge," "The Bridge for Change," and "The Cost of the Problem" (the consultant). The common thread is thinking like a business person, not a salesperson.

Bottom line, the stance and the point of view about selling you'll find in this book isn't really about selling at all. It's about how mature, intelligent, and ethical human beings would interact with each other to assure each other's success. And that's what makes this book really radical, refreshing, and required. Enjoy the ride!

JOHN SULLIVAN, PHD
Learning Partners, Inc.

Acknowledgments

Looking back on 30-plus years of business, which includes 21 years since founding Prime Resource Group, I undoubtedly have many individuals to thank for their contributions and support. I first thank my partner in 33 years of marriage and five businesses, Pat Thull. I realize the concept of being partners in marriage and in business intrigues many and is unimaginable to others. I can describe our partnership only as "as good as it gets." Pat has been an integral and driving force behind the growth of our organization and the development of the Prime Process. She is a student of the process and a master of the complex sale. She has brought in and served multiple clients in her role as vice president of sales and marketing and now COO of Prime Resource Group. Her editorial contribution has had a significant impact on the clarity of this book.

I thank my parents, who instilled an attitude of accomplishment and continually encouraged and supported my earliest entrepreneurial pursuits. My father provided a role model that I found reflected repeatedly in many successful sales professionals I have met. He sold industrial building granite for 35 years and sold to executives of some of the most admired corporations in America and through some of the most well-known architects in this country. I have a vivid memory of taking a business trip with him when I was 12 years old. I witnessed the respect he had for his clients and the reciprocal respect they showed him. I was immediately struck with the greatness of his profession. I am most grateful that my dad lived to see the beginnings of Diagnostic Selling and the success of Prime Resource Group.

The list of clients and associates that have contributed to the evolution of this process is long, starting with my first sales manager, Al Miller, and my first business mentor, Bob New. Two valued clients were Ken Bozevich and Lovell Baker, 3M managers, who took a calculated risk on a "radical" new sales program and a young consultant some 20 years ago. I thank Al Eggert, Ben Michelson, and Dave Madsen, of 3M HIS, who built and supported one of the most successful implementations of the Prime Process. I am grateful also to Peter Muldowney, Terry Slattery, Bob Groening, Gerhard Meese, Don Beveridge, Bill Graham, Nido Quebien, Rob Castien, Bob Brockman, Richard Brooks, Per Lofving, Ilan Shanon, Charlie Morris, Robin Wolfson, and John Willig.

The early development of this material began with the creation of our Diagnostic Selling program and was assisted by a gifted editor and writer, Tom Watson. John Sullivan, PhD, and Judy Robinson, PhD, have provided invaluable support with their expertise in instructional design and curriculum development to capture the Diagnostic Business Development Process and turn it into a replicable process that has been embraced across multiple industries and cultures.

We began this project knowing I would need serious "adult supervision" to keep on track and sift through mountains of information, research, and experiences to distill a topic as broad as "Mastering the Complex Sale" into a single book. We thank Ted and Donna Kinni for doing just that. Their expert assistance in crafting our story has been impressive and enjoyable.

And thanks to the entire team at John Wiley & Sons, Matt Holt, our editor, and the great publicity support from Celia Rocks and Dottie DeHart.

A special thank you goes to Jennifer, Jessica, and Brian.

Contents

Introduction

Today's turbulent marketplace creates constant competitive movement, fluctuating threats, and lucrative opportunities. To acquire, expand, and retain long-term profitable customer relationships, companies and individuals cannot rely on a conventional approach to sales. Increased complexity, escalating customer requirements, rapid commoditization, and relentless competitive forces are all putting intense pressure on sales and marketing, demanding superior strategies and precise execution. Sales success requires an integrated process that enables you to respond within limited windows of opportunity.

To compete and win more sales in the world of complex sales, sales and marketing professionals need a way to work smarter. They need a new business paradigm that is specifically designed for the *complex sales* arena, one that offers a system *and* the skills and the mental discipline needed to execute it. That smarter way to sell is the subject of this book—called Diagnostic Business Development, or the Prime Process.

A smarter way to sell should transform the conventional sales pitch that customers must endure into a high quality decision-making process that customers value. The Prime Process equips salespeople with a way to help customers discover, diagnose, design, and deliver the best possible solution to their problems.

A smarter way to sell should transform salespeople from predators into valued business partners in the customer's mind. The Prime Process positions salespeople as professionals who bring credibility, integrity, and dependability to the business engagement. They are a source of business advantage to their customers.

A smarter way to sell should transform the sales process from premature presentations, pleas for customer consideration, to a process of mutual confirmation. The Prime Process builds mutual understanding step by step, thus ensuring that both sales professionals and their customers most efficiently use their resources.

A smarter way to sell should transform the conventional solutions-based, seller-first approach to sales into a diagnostic-based, customer-centric approach. The Prime Process enables salespeople to differentiate themselves from their competitors in the most effective way of all—by standing squarely on the customer's side of the engagement.

In fact, a smarter way to sell is to *stop selling* in the conventional sense. Instead, we need to think in terms of business development, that is, developing our customer's business.

We need to get beyond selling to managing decisions. All good salespeople have a sales process, all customers have a buying process, and they typically have conflicting objectives. We need to set aside conventional processes and replace them with a collaborative decision process, provided by the sales professional.

We need to get beyond problem solving to managing change. Providing quality solutions to customer problems no longer assures a successful sale and certainly does not guarantee a successful implementation of that solution. Change, along

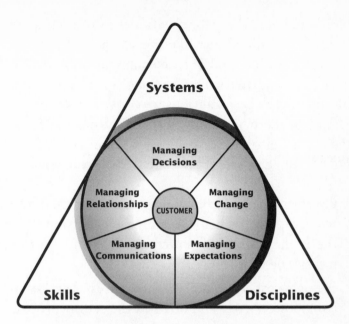

Beyond Selling to Business Development®

with all the attendant risks involved, is the key issue customers face. We need to help them understand and navigate the change required to assure a successful implementation of our solutions.

We need to get beyond meeting needs to managing expectations. Just because we see a need does not mean that our customers see it or understand it as clearly as we do. We need to evolve and expand our customers' understanding of their needs and their expectations about solutions.

We need to get beyond transactions to managing relationships. In the rush to close deals, we too often forget the human factor and squander the long-term opportunity. We need to address the hopes, fears, and aspirations of our customers and create mutually beneficial relationships.

Finally, we need to get beyond reacting to managing clear communications. Too often, we react to customers in rote patterns, without asking for clarification or thinking deeper. As a result, we sound just like every other salesperson. We need to achieve the kind of true communication that fosters crystal-clear and mutual understanding of our customers' problems and the best solutions we can recommend.

Among the byproducts of this fundamental reframing of the methodology of the complex sale are solutions to some of today's toughest sales challenges. The Prime Process:

- Gives salespeople a proven, repeatable method for gaining access to and managing multiple decision makers at the highest levels of power and influence in the customer's organization.

- Helps salespeople to set themselves apart from the competition early and often in the selling process.

- Offers a way to get on the winning track in the sales process and to dramatically reduce the sales cycle time.

- Eliminates the trap of "unpaid consulting."

- Equips salespeople to identify untapped sources of opportunity and develop new business instead of chasing the usual suspects along with the rest of the crowd.

- Provides a common process and language with which the entire sales, marketing, and support team can present a unified voice to the customer and effectively *Diagnose, Design*, and *Deliver* optimal solutions.

What this book promises its readers is a pragmatic exploration of the complex sales world and an optimal approach to mastering and winning the complex sale. We're confident we can deliver on that promise because of the success our clients have achieved through Diagnostic Business Development.

1

The World in Which We Sell

Converging Forces of Rapid Commoditization and Increasing Complexity

Survival in today's sophisticated marketplace requires us to overcome two opposing forces: (1) increasing complexity and (2) rapid commoditization, the pressure from buyers to devalue the differences between goods and services and reduce their decision to the lowest common denominator—the selling price (see Figure 1.1). Let's be direct: The world in which we sell is being pulled apart by these two opposing forces. Even our most complex solutions are at the mercy of commoditization as our customers, swimming in a haze of confusion and performance pressure, grapple with tough decisions impacting their responsibilities. The net effect is a deadly spiral of shrinking profit margins.

Seeking competitive differentiation through increasing uniqueness and complexity is a deadly double-edged sword. These competitive advantages rapidly erode as they

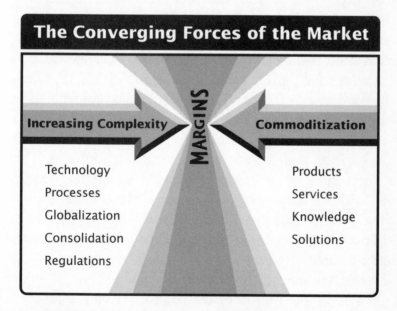

FIGURE 1.1 The Converging Forces of the Market

surpass the customers' level of comprehension. As this occurs, the overwhelming tendency of the customer is to treat all solutions the same—as a commodity.

With a true commodity, price and total transaction cost are the driving forces in the marketplace. As commoditization occurs, sales skills become less and less effective and transactional efficiency becomes the critical edge. The professional salesforce itself soon becomes a luxury that is too expensive to maintain. If your company has chosen to embrace commoditization as a dedicated strategy, it is—or soon will be—pursuing the lowest transactional cost it can achieve, and a book on sales process and skills will not be of much value.

When there is *increasing complexity*, sophistication, innovation, and value realized are the driving forces in the marketplace. To survive, a company is required to recruit and equip sales professionals who are capable of understanding the complex situations their customers face, configuring the complex solutions offered by their companies, and managing the complex relationships that are required to bring them both together. In short, the ability to create value for customers and capture value for companies is the key. Thus, the good news is that the future of the sales profession is secure in the complex environment. The bad news is that as your company brings increasingly complex offerings to the marketplace, your customers are being left confused. They are less and less able to understand the situations they face and evaluate these complex solutions, which tends to limit their decision-making criteria to the simplest elements of your offering, the lowest common denominators—price and specifications. If complexity accurately characterizes your selling environment, this book is for you.

We see the impact of the complexity challenge every day. My colleagues and I spend thousands of hours each year teaching and coaching salespeople internationally. We meet the cream of the crop, the people who sell complex and costly solutions in a wide range of industries, including, but not limited to, professional and financial services, software, medical devices and equipment, IT solutions, industrial chemicals, and manufacturing systems. The value of the individual sales they undertake ranges from tens of thousands of dollars to tens of millions of dollars. These sales professionals are highly educated, very sophisticated, and definitely street-smart. And they are well paid. They are levels above the stereotypic image of salespeople that is imprinted on the public imagination.

Even though these professionals are masters of their crafts, we hear them express their frustration about the outcome of their efforts on a regular basis. The most common lament we hear is one that we've labeled the *Dry Run*. The generic version goes like this:

> *A prospective customer contacts your company with a problem that your solutions are expressly designed to address. A salesperson or team is assigned the account. The customer is qualified, appointments are set, and your sales team interviews the customer's team to determine what they want, what their requirements are, and what they plan to invest. A well-crafted, multimedia presentation is created, a complete solution within the customer's budget is proposed, and all the customer's likely questions are answered. Everyone on the customer's side of the table smiles and nods at the conclusion of the formal proposal. Everything makes good business sense. Your solution fills the customer's needs. You believe the sale is "in the bag," but the decision to move forward never comes. The result after weeks, months, and, sometimes, years of work: no sale. The customer doesn't buy from your company and often doesn't buy from your competitors. The worst-case scenario ends in what we refer to as* unpaid consulting. *The customer takes your solution design, shops it down the street, and does the work themselves*

or buys from a competitor. Many times, the customer simply doesn't take action on a solution that it needs and can afford. This, with a twist here and there, is the Dry Run. *Sure, it's great practice and it's great experience, but this isn't a training exercise. This is the real world of selling, and, in this world, it's your job to bring in the business.*

What's going on in this story? The sales team is doing everything it has been taught, but the result is not what is expected. In fact, our experiences with more than 10,000 salespeople each year suggest that, in the complex environment, the outcome of the conventional sales process is increasingly random and unpredictable. We have already hinted at some of the reasons behind this dilemma, but to truly understand the situation, we examine the nature of the complex sale itself.

The Mother of All Procurements

Complex sales are primarily business-to-business and business-to-government transactions. They involve multiple people, with multiple perspectives, often multiple companies, and frequently cross multiple cultural and country borders. The complex sales cycle can run from days to years. Undertaking this level of sale requires significant investment in time and resources.

The $200 billion defense contract that Lockheed Martin won in 2001 may well be the largest complex sale in history. Granted, few companies will ever compete for a sale of this magnitude. However, even though this is an extreme example of a complex sale, it does share common characteristics with all complex sales.

This contract grew out of the U.S. Defense Department's Joint Strike Fighter (JSF) program, which was conceived in the early 1990s. The Pentagon decided to replace the aging fighter fleets in all branches of the nation's military with a next-generation jet that could be built on a standardized product platform and that combined the features of a stealth aircraft with state-of-the-art supersonic capabilities. In 1995, the United Kingdom jumped into the project when it decided that the fighters in the Royal Air Force and Navy also needed replacing and that the JSF program would be the most economical way to accomplish that task. Today, at least six other countries, including the Netherlands, Italy, Denmark, Norway, Canada, and Turkey, are considering participation.

The contract to design and manufacture jets for the JSF program was so large that it caused a fundamental reconfiguration in the aerospace industry. In fact, the winner of the contract would become the nation's only fighter jet manufacturer. Now-retired Lockheed aeronautics executive James "Micky" Blackwell called it "the mother of all procurements" and suggested that the JSF program would eventually be worth $1 trillion to whichever company won it.[1] In 1996, when the Pentagon announced that Lockheed Martin and Boeing had each won a $660 million prototype development contract and would be the only companies allowed to compete for the program's final contract, one competitor, McDonnell Douglas Corporation, sold itself to Boeing. Northrop Grumman, another spurned competitor, tried to merge with Lockheed Martin; after the government blocked that deal, Northrop Grumman declared it would no longer compete as a prime contractor in the military aerospace market and joined the Lockheed team as a partner.

In October 2001, the final contract, the largest single defense deal ever, was awarded to Lockheed. It called for the eventual delivery of more than 3,000 aircraft to the U.S. military alone, and the Congressional Budget Office valued it at $219 billion over 25 years. That seems to be the tip of the iceberg: The company will easily export another 3,000 planes, and the life of the contract could extend into the middle of this century. Revenue generated by this sale may not hit the trillion-dollar mark that Micky Blackwell targeted, but based on sales of past generations of fighter jets, industry analysts think that it could easily reach three-quarters of that figure.

We've already mentioned the first two characteristics that all complex sales share with the JSF contract. Complex sales involve large financial investments and long sales cycles. Case in point: JSF's several hundred billion dollar price tag and the years that it took to award the final contract.

Another common characteristic of the complex sale is that it requires multiple decisions at multiple levels in the customer's organization. It frequently involves multiple organizations working with the customer. In the purchase of many products and services, the buying decision is clear and entails little risk. The customer clearly understands the problem, clearly understands the solution, and can easily sort through the pros and cons of each alternative. There really is not much that can go wrong that would not be anticipated.

In the complex sale, there is no single buying decision or single decision maker. The buying process is actually a long chain of interrelated decisions, impacting multiple departments and multiple disciplines that can ripple throughout a customer's organization. In the JSF program, this chain of decisions stretched beyond the horizon. It included a huge number of decisions with serious implications for the future, such as the decision to pursue a single platform fighter that can be modified for vastly different uses and the decision to award the entire contract to a single prime contractor.

The difficulty of coping with the long decision chain is compounded by another common characteristic of the complex sale: multiple decision makers. Shelves of books are devoted to helping salespeople find and close *the* decision maker, that one person who can make the decision to buy on the spot. In the case of a commodity sale, there often is just such a person—a purchasing agent or a department head with a budget or senior executive who can simply sign a deal.

In the complex sale, however, the search for this mythical buyer is fruitless. There is no single decision maker; often, even the CEO cannot make a unilateral decision and must defer to the board of directors. Certainly, there is always a person who can say yes when everyone else says no, and, conversely, there is always someone who can say no when everyone else says yes. Today, the majority of decisions, quality decisions, are the result of a consensus-building effort—an effort that the best of sales professionals orchestrates. Therefore, the complex sale has multiple decision makers, each seeing the issues of the transaction from his or her own perspective and each operating in the context of his or her job responsibilities and their own self-interest. The decision makers in a complex sale may be spread throughout an organization and represent different functions and frequently will have conflicting objectives. They can be spread throughout the world, as in the case of a multinational corporation, buying products and services that will be used throughout its organization. They may also represent multiple organizations, as in the JSF contract, where the different sectors of the military, the executive branch, and the Congress were all involved in the sale, as well as the governments and military forces of other nations.

The complex sale, however, is not a run-of-the-mill transaction. The customer's situation is often a rarely encountered or a unique occurrence. The advent of e-commerce brought about just such a situation. Suddenly, an entirely new distribution channel became available to corporations, institutions, and governments. Many organizations floundered as they tried in vain to understand this new world. Should they go online or not? What would happen if they did? What would happen if they didn't?

Organizations that did make a decision to expand on-line were faced with a second set of critical decisions. The solutions themselves were based on newly developed technology, and customers had few guidelines for judging between them. The results, as anyone who watched the rise and subsequent fall of the e-commerce revolution knows, were widely varied. But one thing is certain: For each successful online expansion, there were hundreds of equally spectacular failures.

If you examine the JSF program, you find that the Pentagon invested years in exploring and defining the problems of its existing fighter fleets. It determined the two companies most likely to create the best solutions to those problems and paid them $1.32 billion to develop prototypes. Only then did they make a final decision.

A final characteristic of the complex sale and major consideration for sales success is that customers require outside assistance or outside expertise to guide them through complex decisions. They cannot do this by themselves. You should begin to consider this question: To what degree do you and your team provide this expertise? To help organize your thoughts, consider that your customers need this expertise in one or more of three major areas.

First, they may require outside expertise to help *Diagnose* the situation. They may not have the ability to define the problem they are experiencing or the opportunity they are missing. In many cases, they may not even recognize there is a problem. So consider: To what degree do you and your team assist the customer in completing a more thorough *Diagnosis*?

Second, even if your customers could accurately diagnose their situations, they may not be able to *Design* the optimal solution. They may not know what options exist, how they would interact, how they might integrate into their current systems, and other such considerations. To what extent do you and your team enable customers to design comprehensive solutions?

Finally, even if your customers could *Diagnose* their problems completely and *Design* optimal solutions, they may not have the ability to implement the solutions and *Deliver* the expected results to their organizations. To what degree do you and your team provide implementation support to assure that the maximum impact of your solutions is achieved?

In summary, the characteristics of complex sales involve long sales cycles. They require multiple decisions that are made by multiple people at multiple levels of power and influence, each of whom approaches the transaction from his or her own perspective. Finally, they involve complicated situations and sophisticated and expensive solutions that are difficult for the customer to understand, evaluate, and implement.

In addition to the elements of the complex sale itself, the two environmental forces that we introduced at the beginning of this chapter—commoditization and increasing complexity—also have a direct effect on sales success. To round out the portrait of the world in which we sell, we take a closer look at each.

Driving Forces of Commoditization

Commoditization is a big word for a phenomenon that salespeople face every day, that is, the pressure from the customer to devalue the differences between their goods and services and reduce their decision to the lowest common denominator—the selling price. The pressure to treat all entries in a category of products and services as identical is driven, in some instances, by very real forces and, in others, by emotional needs. In either case, the pressure exists and sales professionals must deal with it.

Technology is one of the real forces driving commoditization. A good example of how emerging technology can commoditize a product is the personal computer and development of electronic commerce. Before the Internet, enterprise-level personal computer (PC) sales were considered complex sales and all the major computer manufacturers had large sales organizations dedicated to that task. Today, a large portion of those sales positions have been eliminated. PC makers still maintain salesforces for their high-volume customers, but buying a number of PCs for a company can also be accomplished in a self-service, commodity-based transaction.

Even a short visit to a Web site such as Dell.com makes the point abundantly clear. Dell Computer Corporation has played a leading role in the commoditization of the PC and has profited handsomely from its work. The company was founded on a direct-to-the-customer model that eliminated the external sales and distribution chains that other PC manufacturers depended on. When e-commerce technology appeared, Dell was the first to move online. Starting in 1996, Dell customers who wanted a self-serve transaction could research, configure, and price their PCs, associated hardware, and off-the-shelf software on the company's Web site. Today, they can do the same at two or three of Dell's major competitors. They can compare prices and make their purchases without ever speaking to a salesperson. What was once solely considered a complex product (and sale) has been transformed by experience, knowledge, and technology into a product (and sale) that can just as easily be treated as a commodity.

Dell has successfully created the best of all worlds. For the customers who can determine their own needs, configure the computer they want, and set up and use the computer without assistance, Dell has provided the lowest cost of manufacturing in the industry and has enabled its customer to order a computer with little or no sales support. On the other end of the spectrum, for the customer looking to set up an elaborate network of PCs or for a complex e-commerce business, Dell has assembled a team that can provide high-level support in *Diagnosing, Designing,* and *Delivering* sophisticated solutions.

The second real force driving commoditization is the lack of differentiation between competing products in the marketplace. The growing similarity between the products and services that compete in specific market niches is not a figment of our imaginations.

To return for a moment to the personal computer, corporate buyers often see little difference between one company's PCs and the products of its major competitors. Who can blame them? Perhaps the shape and color of the computer is different; so is the name on the box. But, the main components of the computer—the processors, memory, disk drives, and motherboards—are often identical. Therefore, many buyers make this purchase decision based on price.

The similarity between competing products and services is a function of industry response times. Unless they are protected by law (as in the case of new prescription drugs), the length of time that the inventors of new products and services enjoy the advantage of being first into the market is getting shorter and shorter. Competitors see a successful or improved product and quickly match it. Therefore, one important reason for the increasing difficulty in differentiating products and services is that, in actuality, they are increasingly similar.

Another reason it is getting tougher to differentiate products and services is that customers don't want to differentiate them. The more complex products and services are, the more difficult it is for customers to compare and evaluate them. Analyzing and deciding between long lists of nonidentical features is hard. Simply comparing the purchase prices is much easier. Customers, by the way, are the third driving force of commoditization.

Customers are always trying to level the playing field. They attempt to reduce complex sales to their lowest common denominators for good reasons. The most obvious is financial. When customers are able to convince vendors that their offerings are essentially the same, they exert tremendous downward pressure on the price. For instance, if General Electric's jet engines are the same price as Rolls Royce's jet engines and the customer can't or won't see any difference between the two, what must those vendors do to win the sale? Unfortunately, the easiest answer, and the one that takes the least skill to execute, is to cut the price, which is why so much margin erosion occurs at the point of sale.

An example of the extreme impact this can have on a business involves a client who came to us after their business had taken a devastating hit. This company had developed a manufacturing technology that became a standard in the chip manufacturing industry. They produced a piece of capital equipment, sold about 300 units per year, and enjoyed a very large market share. The situation was too good to be true, and a competitor entered the marketplace offering the "same thing" for 32 percent less. The original manufacturer did not initiate the diagnostic process we describe and, faced with the threat of losing customers, lowered prices in response. Their average selling price dropped by 30 percent during the following year, resulting in a reduction of $24 million in margins. The irony of the story is the upstart competitor, who made the claims, sold only 15 units, a 5 percent market share. The manufacturer's inability to respond in a more productive manner nearly destroyed their business.

Customers also try to oversimplify complex transactions for emotional reasons. Often they are in denial about the extent of their problems. Think in personal terms: If your stomach burns and you chew an off-the-shelf antacid, your problem must be temporary and is easily solved. If you go to your doctor, who discovers you have an ulcer, your problem jumps to an entirely different level.

Fear drives customers to oversimplify transactions. Our customers are professionals, and it is difficult for professionals to admit that they don't understand problems and/or solutions. We need to take into account that our customers may be concerned about appearing less than competent in front of us and in front of their bosses. So, instead of asking questions when they don't understand something, they may simply nod and reduce the transaction to what they do understand—the purchase price.

Finally, there is the emotional issue of control. We regret the negative stereotype of a professional salesperson that exists in many customers' minds. Customers are fearful that by acknowledging complexity and admitting their own lack of understanding, they lose control of the transaction and open themselves to manipulative sales techniques. The simpler the customers can make a sale, the less they must depend on salespeople to help them. This is their way to maintain control of the transaction and protect themselves from unprofessional sales tactics.

Driving Forces of Complexity

The portrait of the world in which we sell is almost complete. We have examined the nature of the complex sale and the environmental pressures that are forcing them into commodity-like transactions. The last element in the picture is an equal and opposing pressure that, in essence, is forcing additional complexity into already-complex transactions. Simply put, environmental forces are adding more complexity to the mix. We are seeing complexity piled on complexity.

Many of the driving forces of complexity are emerging from the changing nature of business itself. The structure of our organizations is becoming more complex. In many cases, decentralized organizational structures have replaced the fixed, hierarchical infrastructures on which traditional companies were built. In other cases, consolidations are having the opposite effect and have taken decisions away from the technical, clinical, and operational levels to professional managers who frequently take a vital but limited financial view to their decisions. In addition, the speed with which these transformations are occurring is unprecedented. The result is increasing difficulty in understanding and navigating our way through a customer's business. Identifying the powers of decision and influence in today's corporate labyrinths isn't easy either. With increasing frequency, the customers themselves cannot define their decision process.

The trend toward globalization is exacerbating the growing complexity of organizational structure. We are often selling into decentralized companies that span the globe and encompass dozens of different languages and cultures. "Where in the world are the decision makers?" is not a rhetorical question in an increasing number of situations.

The restructuring of organizations has extended back down the supply chain. Customers are consolidating, fewer companies are controlling higher percentages of demand, and fewer competitors are controlling higher percentages of supply. It's an environment where the winner takes a substantial share, if not all, of the marketplace.

At the same time that our customers are demanding commodity-based pricing from us, they are demanding more complex relationships with us. They are drastically reducing their supply bases and asking the remaining vendors to take a more active role in their business process. They want those of us who are left to become business partners and open our organizations to them. They are also asking us to add value at much deeper levels than we have traditionally delivered to their organizations.

The customers' desire to build tighter bonds with fewer vendors is adding complexity to the sales process. Buying decisions include more considerations and more players, and those players are often located at higher levels in the organization. This is on top of the multiple decisions and multiple decision makers that already characterize complex transactions.

There is an even more sobering consideration here: If your customers are tightening up their supply chain, there will be fewer opportunities in the long run. One lost sale in this environment could easily translate to the long-term loss of the customer. We saw an extreme example of what that can mean in the case of the Pentagon's contract for the Joint Strike Fighter. The companies that did not win that sale had to either abandon that business or accept supporting roles working for the winner. How many customers can you afford to lose on a long-term basis?

Increasing levels of complexity can also be found in the situations and problems our customers face and in the solutions that we offer them. We tend not to see the world through our customers' eyes, but when we do, we find that they face many problems. Their business environments are more competitive than ever, technological advances are radically altering their industries and markets, and their margins for error are always shrinking. The increased complexity of the environment translates directly to increased complexity in their problems.

The solutions that we design to address those problems are correspondingly complex. Products and services must be designed to transcend geographical borders and connect and integrate decentralized structures. Our solutions need to incorporate complex technical innovations and address the needs created by technological change. In addition, our margins for error are always shrinking. The complex solution and the situation it is designed to address are ever changing and increasingly complex.

Finally, complexity is driven by competition. To stay on top of our markets, we often find ourselves trapped in "innovation races" with our competitors; in doing so, we can actually outrun the needs of our customers. Harvard Business School professor Clayton Christensen calls this *performance oversupply* and describes the phenomenon in his book, *The Innovator's Dilemma:* "In their efforts to stay ahead by developing competitively superior products, many companies don't realize the speed at which they are moving up-market, oversatisfying the needs of their original customers as they race the competition toward higher-performance, higher-margin markets."[2]

Ironically, when the complexity that we add to our products and services exceeds the needs of our customers, they respond by ignoring the features they do not need and by treating our offerings as if they were commodities. Here's how Christensen traces the process: "When the performance of two or more competing products has improved beyond what the market demands, customers can no longer base their choice on which is the higher performing product. The basis of product choice often evolves from functionality to reliability, then to convenience, and, ultimately, to price."[3] Here is yet another example of technological innovation driving commoditization.

There are two points to all of this: First, if you are already involved in complex sales, you can expect them to get more complex. Second, if you are not selling a simple commodity but have a relatively simple sale at this time, you may well end up with a full-blown complex sale in the near future.

Getting Back to the *Dry Run*

Now that we have a complete picture of the world in which we sell, we can turn back to the *Dry Run*. In every variation of that scenario, sales professionals are doing everything they have been taught, they are offering high quality, cost-effective solutions, and yet their conversion rate of proposals to sales is in free fall. Why?

The answer is that the nature of the complex sale and the opposing environmental forces of commoditization and complexity are making it extraordinarily difficult not just for sales professionals to bring in revenues, but for customers to fully understand the problems and opportunities that they face. The complex sale and the forces that affect it are impairing our customers' ability to make rational purchasing decisions. Ultimately, that is why the salespeople in the *Dry Run* did not win the sale. Their customers were unable to make a high-quality decision.

We are not saying the customers are incompetent, although many frustrated salespeople level that charge. The vast majority of customers are fully capable of understanding complex transactions. The problem is they don't have a process that can help them interconnect the key elements of their business to bring the required perspectives together to enable them to make sense of these transactions. That is the underlying thesis of this book and the key insight that allows us to get inside the complex sale: *Customers*

*do not have the depth of experience and knowledge in each of nu-
merous complex subjects that allows them to form high-quality
decision-making processes, which are specific to the requirements
of each and every purchase of complex goods and services.* In complex decisions, one size *does not* fit all.

The often ignored reality of the complex sales environment is that our customers need help. They need help understanding the problems that they face. They need help
designing the optimal solutions to those problems, and they
need help implementing those solutions. The next logical
question is: What can we, as sales professionals, do about it?
The obvious answer is to provide the help our customers
need. But, unfortunately, that isn't the strategy taken by the
majority of the leaders of sales organizations.

By and large, traditional sales leaders are focused on
sales numbers, not the reasons behind them. They understand numbers very well and, like everybody else, they
know that selling is a numbers game. So, the answer that we
usually hear can be summarized in two words: *Sell harder.*
They try to solve the problem by pumping up the system.
They command their troops to make more cold calls, set
more appointments, give more presentations, overcome
more objections, and, thus, close more sales. If the company's conversion rate on proposals is 10 percent, they will
simply write and present more proposals.

We've already described one problem with the "sell
harder" solution. In today's environment, the number of
potential sales is not infinite. At some point, you run out
of viable opportunities and are forced to start chasing more
and more marginal prospects. The other, more fundamental problem with "selling harder" to win the complex sale is
that it fits the popular definition of insanity: You are doing
the same thing repeatedly and expecting a different result.
In the next chapter, we show you why that is so.

2

Trapped in the Conventional Sales Paradigm

*It's Not about Selling—It's about
Managing Quality Decisions*

Prospect, qualify, present, and close—these are the basic elements of the conventional sales process that most sales organizations and salespeople still follow today. The conventional sales process is the most widely used selling paradigm for good reason: It works. That is, it works if you have a simple sale.

In a simple sale, there is a single decision maker faced with an easily understood problem or opportunity and a just-as-easily understood solution. Your task as a sales professional in a simple sale includes finding that buyer, completing a needs analysis, presenting your offering, and convincing the potential customer that it is the best solution available. The conventional sales process is perfectly aligned to meet those requirements.

Think of the mass production, assembly line process Henry Ford invented to make automobiles at the beginning of the last century. It was a remarkable and historical advance that changed the very structure of manufacturing. But what would happen if you reproduced that first assembly line in a modern auto plant? It would be hopelessly outdated and inefficient in this era of robotics and computerized control systems. Most salespeople today face a similar dilemma. The environment in which they sell has evolved, but the selling process that most use has not kept pace and adapted to the new realities.

What happens when you apply the conventional sales process to a complex sale? Now you are dealing with complex problems and correspondingly complex solutions that involve multiple decisions and multiple decision makers. Your customers are also wrestling with more complex problems, and it becomes increasingly difficult for customers to understand and manage the scope, details, and ramifications of their problems and the characteristics of the solutions that will best resolve them. While customers grapple with these issues and before they have a deep understanding of the problems and optimal solutions, conventional salespeople are busy pitching their products and services.

When salespeople use the conventional sales process in a complex situation, they are like major league pitchers hurling 90 mile per hour fastballs at batters who may be at the plate for the very first time or who hit only infrequently. What are the chances that such batters will connect? Likewise, in complex sales, customers don't get up to bat that often. Yet, salespeople continue to pitch reams of solution data at customers, leaving them to comprehend, sort, and connect all of that information on their own. Major league pitchers are trying to make the batter miss. Salespeople want the customer to connect. However, they are depending on their customers' ability to connect their problems to the proposed solutions. When customers strike out, salespeople lose. If your proposal conversion rate is less than 30 percent or if your cost of sales is otherwise unacceptable, chances are good you are striking out too many customers. You are trapped in the conventional sales paradigm.

When you follow the conventional sales process in a complex sale, you run head first into a series of traps that grows progressively more difficult to avoid and that makes a positive outcome for the sale less likely. This downward spiral starts with a fundamental and, as we soon see, erroneous assumption of the conventional sales paradigm—that your customers have a quality decision process with which to diagnose their problems and evaluate your solution. If that's actually the case, the sale should be straightforward. You develop a compelling proposal, answer the customer's final questions, and ask for the sale. The best solution in the marketplace wins. But what if the customer does not have a quality decision process in place?

The Assumption Trap

Conventional selling, on which many of today's most popular sales methodologies are based, depends on the ability of salespeople to determine the customer's decision process. These programs instruct sales professionals to find out what customers are looking for, what's important to them, what they need, and what criteria they will use to decide the purchase. That accomplished, they are directed to create a match between their solutions and customers' buying processes.

We regularly ask the participants in our "Mastering the Complex Sale" seminars to raise their hands if this accurately describes what they have been taught and are encouraged to do and, invariably, the room is full of hands held high. Then, we ask the participants to keep their hands up if they think that their customers have a high-quality decision process for evaluating their specific technology or complex offering. Seldom is a single hand left in the air. The disconcerting realization flashes from face to face: If our customers don't have a high-quality decision process, why are we trying to understand it and fit into it?

The problems resulting from deficiencies in a customer's decision process are further compounded by the tendency of the conventional selling approach to overlook the distinction between the customer's decision process and the customer's approval process. Customers always bring an approval process, they seldom bring a quality decision process. The failure to recognize the differences and treat them as one and the same leads to many *Dry Runs*.

Reality Check
Is There a Quality Decision Process?

Do your customers have a well-defined decision-making process in place that enables them to comprehend the value of your unique offering?

Can you separate the customer's decision process from their approval process?

You can get an accurate sense of the state of customer-driven decision making anytime and anywhere salespeople talk business together. How many times have you heard or perhaps said yourself: "My customers just don't get it"? The reality behind that statement of frustration is not too difficult to figure out: Customers don't "get it" for one of two reasons: You are either overestimating the value your solutions bring to the customer or overestimating the customer's ability to comprehend that value.

Assuming that the solution offered actually has value, the flawed logic behind the "Customer doesn't get it" complaint is that the salespeople who say it are, in essence, blaming customers for being unprepared to buy their solutions. They are implying that customers should somehow be ready to effectively analyze and evaluate products and services, such as capital equipment, that they may buy once a year or once every seven years or less. Or, even more illogically, they are assuming that their customers should have a high-quality decision process capable of evaluating leading-edge solutions, which they may never have considered before or which may be appearing in the marketplace for the first time. Technological leaders in all industries are especially vulnerable in the latter scenario. Their greatest challenge is what Geoffrey Moore calls "crossing the chasm" between the small group of visionary customers who immediately see the value of a new solution and customers in the mainstream marketplace who, through no fault of their own, truly don't yet get it. The bridge across the chasm is the quality decision process and a team of skilled professionals to guide the customer.[1]

Unless you think that salespeople are totally unreasonable, we should note that they get snared in this trap for two reasons. First, all of their training is based on the implicit assumption that the customer will bring the decision process to the table. That is the assumption trap. Second, the trap is compounded by the fact that sales professionals further assume that their customers have a much higher level of comprehension than they actually do.

The best salespeople walk into an opportunity at much higher levels of experience than their customers. They know the products and services they are bringing to market inside and out. In addition, they spend most of their time with customers. They see an entire industry, encounter a full range of operational practices, and often become experts in their customers' businesses. When we shadow experienced sales professionals, we often see them size up a customer's situation and needs, seemingly at a glance. But the advanced perspective and comprehension of sales professionals experienced in the complex sale stand in vivid contrast to the perspective of their potential customers.

Reality Check
What Is the Level of Comprehension?

What is your customer's level of comprehension?

How well do customers understand their own problems?

How well do they understand your solutions?

Unfortunately, even the best salespeople may make an unconscious leap of logic by assuming that their customers see the same things that they see and are, therefore, well prepared to understand their own problems and the value of the forthcoming solutions.

We use the Decision Challenge graph to illustrate this basic and often overlooked reality (see Figure 2.1). The graph's horizontal axis represents the customer's position in their decision process. The progression ranges from 0 percent, at which point customers have no idea there is a problem, to midpoint, where they recognize a problem and are actively investigating solutions, to 100 percent, at which point the customer has made the purchase. The graph's vertical axis represents the customer's level of knowledge about the problem and knowledge of possible solutions. At zero, customers have no knowledge of the types of problems they may have or the problems you solve; at the top of the scale, they have complete, or perfect, knowledge

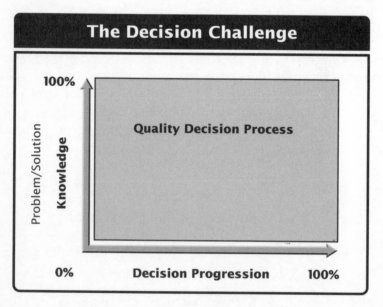

FIGURE 2.1 The Decision Challenge

of their problems and the solutions required to solve them. They know everything needed to make a well-informed, high-quality decision—what to look at and for, what to measure, what to compare, what to test, and so on. Finally, the field of the graph formed by these two axes represents the customer's overall comprehension.

The big question is: Where does your typical customer fall on this graph? More specifically, where does a current client of yours fall? When we conduct this exercise in seminars, we get averages that represent customers in a wide variety of industries. For example, start with the assumption that a customer has entered the market and is actively seeking solutions, knows there is a problem, and has a budget in mind. We place the average customer at 60 percent on the decision axis. Our clients tend to find their customers' knowledge of their problems and possible solutions are less complete. Often, customers have some ideas about the nature of their problems, they may have read

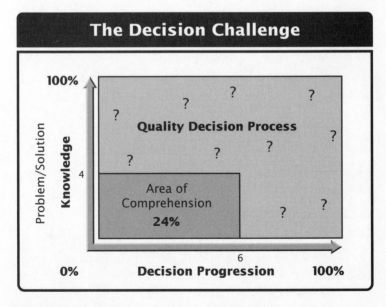

FIGURE 2.2 The Decision Challenge—A Typical Customer

trade publications, spoken to colleagues, and, via the same process, heard a bit about the possible solutions, but they don't have any significant depth of knowledge. Thus, we place them at 40 percent on the knowledge axis. When we plot these points on the graph, this customer's area of comprehension fills just 24 percent of the field (see Figure 2.2 on page 29). If you begin presenting solutions to this customer, he or she will understand only 24 percent of what you say.

In this example, if you attempt to communicate the value of your complex solution, your customer is not going to comprehend about three-quarters of what you say. More accurately, the customer's ability to connect your information to their business is greatly impaired, and they will find it neither useful nor particularly relevant. This miscommunication explains why we see low proposal-to-sales conversion ratios, long sales cycles, and extreme price pressure in complex sales. A customer who cannot comprehend a solution will probably not buy it, will certainly not buy it quickly, and

Reality Check
Are You Exceeding Your Customer's
Level of Comprehension?

How much of your solutions' added value falls inside your customers' area of comprehension?

How much of your company's competitive advantages and value adds fall inside your customers' area of comprehension?

What are the questions your customers do not realize they should be asking about their problems and your solutions?

won't be willing to pay a premium price for it. With a comprehension level that low, every solution looks the same.

The traps in the conventional sales process don't end with flawed assumptions. They are compounded by the primary element of the process itself.

The Presentation Trap

Today's complex sale environment can be characterized by an inordinate preoccupation, even obsession, with the presentation of solutions. Everything salespeople do before—the prospecting, contacting, and qualifying of potential customers—seems to be aimed at creating the opportunity to present their solutions. Everything after—the downhill run to the sale itself that includes overcoming objectives, negotiating, and closing—is designed to support and reiterate the presentation. Accordingly, sales organizations devote tremendous amounts of time and resources to creating compelling presentations and proposals.

The irony is that most of this effort is lost on customers. *Presentations that are too early in complex decisions are largely a waste of time.*

Conventional salespeople hate to hear this; the presentation is the key weapon in their sales arsenal. It is their security blanket, their comfort zone, and they loathe giving it up. "Wait a minute," they protest, "our presentations are aimed at educating customers. They will not buy what they don't understand."

Exactly right, customers will not buy what they don't understand. A presentation *can* lift the customer's level of comprehension. However, it is one of the least effective methods for accomplishing that goal because of three reasons:

1. A presentation, even one that includes advanced multi-media elements, is, in its essence, a lecture. The salesperson is the teacher and the customer is the student. The salesperson teaches by telling. The big problem with teaching by telling is that hardly anyone remembers what they hear. People retain only about 30 percent of what they hear. The use of visual aids (e.g., a PowerPoint slide show) boosts retention rates to 40 percent. But the generally accepted rule of thumb among learning experts is that more than half of even the most sophisticated presentation is lost.[2]

2. A typical sales presentation rarely devotes more than 10 to 20 percent of its focus to the customer and their current situation. Generally, 80 to 90 percent of a typical sales presentation is devoted to describing the salesperson's company, its solutions, and the future being sold. Therefore, while a presentation may raise the customer's comprehension level, that gain is usually centered on the solutions being offered. All too often, salespeople are dealing with customers who are not sure of the exact nature of their problems. Nevertheless, those salespeople are spending most of their time talking about solutions. As a result, while customers may be greatly impressed with the offering

---

Reality Check
Is There a Balance between Timing and Content?

What percentage of your sales presentation/proposal is devoted to describing your company and your solution?

What percentage of your sales presentation/proposal is devoted to describing your customer's business, situation, problem and objectives?

being presented, they still lack a compelling understanding of how it applies to their situation and they do
not know why they should buy it.

3. There is a third compelling reason that presentations
   are a waste of time in complex sales: Your competitors
   are following the same strategy; they are busy presenting, as well. Unless you have no competition, your customers will surely see them. They have meetings set
   up with you and one, two, or even more of your competitors. In each meeting, a sales team is presenting
   the best side of its solutions. Your team is telling the
   customers that they need the solutions that only your
   company offers, and your competitors are making the
   same arguments about their solutions. In every case,
   the presentations are heavily skewed toward the seller
   and the solutions.

Look at this from the customer's perspective. Based on
what we said about the customer's area of comprehension, it
is highly likely that two-thirds or more of the information
that customers hear falls outside their area of comprehension. Further, what they do hear sounds very much the same.
It all deals almost exclusively with solutions and is not connected to their unique situation.

How do customers then respond to competing conventional presentations? They concentrate their efforts on the

Reality Check
Are You Really That Different?

In the eyes of the customer, how different is the structure, format, and content of your sales presentation
from your major competitors' sales presentations?

information that falls inside their area of comprehension. Customers attempt to make the complex understandable by weighing those elements that vendors' offerings have in common and eliminating those elements that do not fit neatly onto an over simplified comparison chart. When this happens, salespeople's ability to differentiate their offering from the competition is subverted, and price, the one common denominator of all offers, again raises its ugly head and is likely to become the deciding factor in the sale.

Customers may also respond by not responding. They listen politely as you "educate" them, thank you for your time, and promise to get back in touch when they are ready to make a decision. This is the setup for the *Dry Run*, as described in Chapter 1.

Finally, some customers may actively respond. They may ask you to justify the information you have presented or challenge the viability of your solution. This is the response set that every conventional salesperson is expecting. The customer objects and the sales professional goes to work overcoming those objections. It is a time-honored element of selling, and it contains the final, major trap of the conventional sales process.

The Adversarial Trap

When salespeople start "overcoming objections," they are placing, by definition, themselves in conflict with their customers. At best, this sets the stage for polite disagreements and respectful differences of opinion. At worst, it turns the sales process into a battle in which the seller must somehow conquer the buyer to win the sale. You can hear this in the language that appears so often in sales training and in the conversations between salespeople and their managers. Words such as *persist, insist, persuade,* and *convince* all imply aggressive behavior.

This problem is inherent in the conventional sales process. Because it focuses solely on making the sale, any reluctance on the part of the customer translates into a direct threat to the salesperson's success.

The conflict between buyer and seller is exacerbated by the frustration that results from the miscommunication engendered by the conventional process. Salespeople are presenting professionally packaged data complete with executive summaries that their prospective customers find either unintelligible or unconnected to their situation. Confused and with no sound basis on which to evaluate the information, customers respond negatively. Conventional salespeople, who are overestimating their customers' level of comprehension, interpret this as an objection to be overcome and swing into action. "No," they say, "you don't get it. You do need our solution and here's why . . ." Now the salespeople are arguing with their customers.

What happens next? If the customers don't shut down the presentation altogether, they may offer a second negative response. Another round of verbal sparring ensues. The customers' frustrations turn into exasperation. But now the sale is in doubt and the salespeople *know* that the customers need the solution, so they escalate their efforts. The downward spiral accelerates. Repeatedly, we have witnessed all of this occur in the most polite and respectful terms. No matter how civilized the exchange, the net result is that the salespeople and the customers have become adversaries. The sale has turned into a battle . . . a battle in which customers always have the final say.

There are unfortunate exceptions, but, for the most part, salespeople using a conventional approach aren't

Reality Check
Are You Challenging or Collaborating?

Do you find yourself debating with customers?

Are your customers reacting defensively and/or challenging your recommendations?

How much of your time with customers is spent presenting, persuading, and convincing?

purposely trying to beat up their customers. They are simply following the accepted dictates of a conventional sales process that generates statements such as:

- Whether they know it or not, every "qualified" prospect needs your products and services.
- Persuasion is the key quality of successful selling.
- If you are persistent and pursue the customer at regular intervals and with increasing intensity, you will eventually get a sale.
- An objection is a signal that the customer wants to be convinced to buy.
- The real selling doesn't start until the customer says no.

There is a kernel of truth in each of these statements, but they are also the source of many of the sales techniques that customers find most irritating. They turn selling into a game where someone, either seller or buyer, must lose.

We are not saying that the adversarial mind-set won't produce sales. It will. We call it "Sales, James Bond style." Every sales organization has a James or Jamie Bond on the payroll, and too many managers are looking to hire more of them. You can drop the Bond-style salesperson out of an airplane into any territory, any prospect, any product, any quota, and you know they will come back with the business.

There is a problem, however, with the Bond approach. There will be a lot of collateral damage. People are going to get hurt on both sides of the table. Many salespeople, and even managers, try to rationalize this away and depend on their service and support functions to repair the damage. But customer relationships are fragile, memory is long, and customers have options. The service person's saying "I'm sorry, you know how salespeople can be" may not cut it. Further, in the real world of business, where margins are tight and a few percentage points of additional cost turn a profitable order into a loss, the Bond style can quickly become a major liability. Promise what you can't profitably deliver or coerce customers to do something they aren't sure about and you either lose customers or rack up the red ink. With today's instant communications, negative perceptions spread very quickly, which can make new business acquisition more difficult.

Add It Up

We haven't yet exhausted the list of traps in the conventional selling process. There are others, large and small, that negatively impact key performance metrics, such as margins, proposal conversion ratios, sales cycle time, and forecasting accuracy. We discuss more of these in later chapters, but for now, all we need to realize is that the three traps previously described are the fundamental problems facing salespeople who try to impose a traditional sales process on complex problems and solutions.

The first trap of conventional selling causes salespeople to depend on their customers' decision-making processes, which frequently is missing key elements. The belief that customers have a high-quality decision process leads to a second erroneous assumption: Customers' ability to understand their own problems and evaluate all the solutions available allows them to discern the true value of the salesperson's unique solutions.

These assumptions cause salespeople to fall into the second trap of conventional sales. Because they assume higher levels of comprehension and decision-making ability on the part of their customers than actually exist, salespeople focus the majority of their efforts on presentation. In doing so, they largely ignore the customers' world, the most significant source of credibility, differentiation, and decision criteria in any sale—thus creating a major disconnect between customers and solutions. The strategy to compete at the solutions level and the rush to present information heighten the blur between competing solutions. This reinforces customers' drive toward commoditization by validating their view that we are all the same.

Finally, the emphasis on sales presentations exacerbates the communication gap between buyer and seller, leading to frustration, misunderstandings, conflict, and adversarial relationships—all of which impede the salesperson's ability to create cooperative and trust-based relationships with customers. This schism is the major reason underlying the protective behaviors customers so often adopt when dealing with salespeople.

These problems are what manufacturing quality guru W. Edwards Deming defined as *systemic problems*. We can't solve them by disciplining individual salespeople who step over some arbitrary line. Instead, the process itself causes the problem. The only effective and enduring way to resolve these problems is to set aside the conflicting elements of the conventional selling process. And that is exactly what we propose in the following chapters.

3

A Proven Approach to Complex Sales

You're Either Part of Your System or Somebody Else's

A theory that explains how to sell, or explains anything else for that matter, is a product of abstract reasoning. It is someone's speculation about the nature of an activity or process. A theory may or, as is too often the case, may not be an accurate reflection of its subject's true nature. What grounds a theory and makes it worth adopting and emulating is that it works in everyday practice in the real world. That's why we shadow sales professionals with successful track records in complex sales.

Our clients repeatedly ask us to research and explain what makes their best salespeople excel. They request that we capture from their salespeople: What do they do? How do they think? What questions do they ask? What do they say to prospects and customers? How do they handle competitive threats? And when we've distilled it all down, the objective is to teach these best practices to the rest of their sales organization—to replicate the best of the best.

To identify and transfer the best practices in complex sales, we spend roughly one-third of our time consulting in the field. In other words, we work with our customers' top salespeople as they call on their customers. In total, we have accompanied high performers (the top 3 to 5 percent of salespeople) on more than 4,000 appointments. We've watched them work, studied their reasoning and behavior patterns, and have come to understand the thinking and the methods behind their success.

We looked to the sciences of human behavior and interpersonal communication to explain why what we observed was working. In short, we reverse-engineered the success process. We observed what worked, sought out solid research to explain why, and evolved learning and performance development models to explain and teach the process to others.

Shadowing top-performing salespeople quickly led us to a surprising observation: Generally, the most successful don't rely on traditional selling techniques. When we accompany the best of the best on calls, we find that they are not offering their companies' sales brochures. They don't recite prepared pitches chapter and verse, nor do they seem to steer the conversation or lead the customer in any overt manner. We discuss what is going on later in the chapter, but for now, let's just say that top performers are *not* selling . . . at least, not in the conventional sense.

The success of top performers is often a mystery to their employers and their colleagues. They are considered anomalies—rare exceptions to the rule whose success is a natural, but irreproducible, phenomenon. This is compounded by the fact that many top performers can't clearly articulate the reasons behind their own success and rarely follow their companies' standard sales processes. Here's how a typical conversation sounds:

> We ask, "Was there a particular reason you didn't bring out the product brochures on this appointment?"
>
> The answer comes back: "I don't know. They seem to distract the customer."
>
> "In what way?"
>
> "Well, it's too easy to start talking about the product and get a lot of questions."
>
> "Is that a bad thing?"
>
> "I guess not, but I know I don't get the information I need when I spend all my time talking about our

products. I seem to be more effective when I leave the brochures in my office."

These top performers are not being cagey. Rather, they have developed a personal style of selling and a natural communication process through experience. It is often a long and painful period of trial-and-error experimentation. Once success is achieved, there is a tendency to suppress all the pain they went through to perfect the process. Now, they are too busy winning sales to spend time documenting what they are doing and analyzing how and why it works. They are seldom able to explain in a clear fashion why they do what they do and frequently respond: "It just seems to work," or "It felt like that was the right thing to say." Not very instructive. Nevertheless, their hard-won knowledge is an extraordinarily valuable resource as a sound basis for a model of sales excellence.

Over the years, we've worked very hard to translate those "seems" and "felt likes" into tangible and teachable elements. We've distilled the common attributes and behaviors of top performers into three primary areas. We've studied how these three areas connect to research and theories in organizational and behavioral psychology, decision theory, emotional intelligence, interpersonal dynamics, and change management. Based on that knowledge, we developed and refined a complex sales methodology, which is organized into three primary elements—systems, skills, and disciplines:

1. A *system* is a set procedure or organized process that leads to a consistent and predictable result. Systems are the processes that top performers follow to accomplish their goals and the procedures and tools that their organizations provide to support their efforts.

2. *Skills* are the content knowledge along with the physical and mental abilities that enable salespeople to execute the system. Skills are tools and techniques that top performers use to accomplish their goals.

3. *Discipline* is the mind-set of the professional. It is about attitude, standards of performance, and mental and emotional stamina. Disciplines of high-performing sales professionals are the mental and emotional attitudes with which professionals approach their work and the mental or emotional stamina that they draw on to consistently and successfully see it through.

Think of systems as the "what to do," the skills as the "how to," and discipline as the inner strength that supports the "will do."

The knowledge gained from shadowing top sales professionals is organized into these three areas for good reason. Systems, skills, and disciplines are the foundational elements and guiding principles of all professional bodies of knowledge. Professionals such as pilots, accountants, engineers, doctors, and lawyers are called on to learn, practice, and master these three areas. Pilots follow many systems to operate the planes they fly. They master physical and mental skills to execute those systems, and they embrace a discipline or mind-set that governs how they think about their work and provides the mental stamina to remain cool, calm, and collected while performing the critical task at hand. To be able to speak of selling as a profession, which is exactly what we consider it to be, we need to be able to define the systems, skills, and disciplines that must be adopted, consistently practiced, and mastered to achieve its fullest potential.

We begin defining a professional body of knowledge for winning the complex sale by describing the disciplines that top sales professionals bring to their jobs.

A Discipline for Complex Sales

The discipline with which top performing salespeople approach their work is perhaps the most critical component of their success. Just as the assumptions inherent in traditional sales methodology doom those who accept them to ineffectiveness and miscommunication, the mental framework with which we approach the complex sale acts as the enabler of all that follows. Mind-set is the starting gate of complex sales success. Without the mind-set or point of view, the best laid skills or tactics will fall flat on their face.

Three statements summarize, in broad terms, the discipline of complex sales:

1. *The most successful people in complex sales recognize that for their customers, the process of buying goods and services is all about making a decision to change.* When they are working with a customer, they are actually helping that customer navigate through the change process.

All too often, a sales professional uncovers a serious problem the customer is experiencing, which the customer agrees is a problem, and wants to solve. They have discussed the solution options, and the customer agrees that the solution can eliminate the problem, yet they do not buy. Why does this occur? It's not that the customer doesn't have a problem, and it's not that you don't have a solution. It occurs because the customer cannot or will not go through the personal or organizational changes needed to implement the solution.

Every purchase—complex or not—is based on a customer's decision to change. In simple sales, the customer's decision and the change process is often transparent, but it does take place. At a most elemental level, even a purchase of paper for the copy machine involves a degree of change.

"I notice we're out of paper; call my supplier or go to the Web and order the paper and restock the cabinet." The decision was simple—a repeat purchase and not much thought needed to go into it. No muss, no fuss. However, change did take place. I went from no paper to ample supply, I'm more relaxed about the upcoming reports to be copied and distributed, and my bank balance or available budget dropped by a few dollars.

In simple sales, a salesperson can ignore customers' change process, comfortable that customers will navigate the elements of change on their own. Elements of the decision and changes involved with the purchase are clear to the customer. Thus, the customer understands the risk involved in the change, and resistance to making the change is low. But what happens when the complexity of the sale increases in a business-to-business transaction? The decision elements of the situation and the changes involved in the purchase are more complicated and more difficult to understand. The risk of changing is higher. The investment, the requirements of implementation, and the emotional elements—the impact on the buyer's career and livelihood—all create a higher risk of change. Accordingly, resistance to change is substantially higher. Change and risk management now play a major role in the decision and subsequent sale.

The more complex a sale becomes, the more radical the change the customer must undertake and the greater the perceived, as well as actual, risk. A conventional salesperson, who is solely focused on presenting and selling his or her solutions, is ignoring the critical elements of decision, risk, and change in the complex sale. The most successful salespeople, on the other hand, are noted for their ability to understand and guide the customer's change progression (see Figure 3.1).

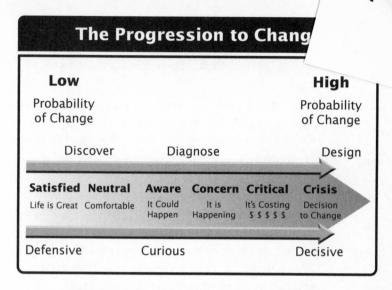

FIGURE 3.1 The Progression to Change

There is a large body of psychological and organizational research concerning the dynamics of change. A key insight is that the decision to change is usually made as a response to negative situations and, thus, is driven by negative emotions. People change when they feel dissatisfied, fearful, and/or pressured by their current problems. Similarly, customers are more likely to buy in those same circumstances. Conversely, people who are satisfied with their current situation are unlikely to change and are unlikely to buy.

The best salespeople understand that all customers are located somewhere along a change spectrum. They work with customers to identify and understand their areas of dissatisfaction, to quantify the dollar impact of the absence of a solution, and to design the optimum solution.

What happens when salespeople ignore the *Progression to Change* (see Table 3.1)? Here is a common scenario: The salesperson focuses on selling the future benefits of his offering. He does a wonderful job presenting, eventually

TABLE 3.1 Progression to Change

Satisfied	"Life is great!" Customers have strong feelings of success. They feel their situation is very good and see no need to change.
Neutral	"I'm comfortable." Customers have no conscious feelings of satisfaction or pain. They are not actively exploring their problems; they are not considering change.
Aware	"It could happen to me." Customers have some discomfort. They understand that a problem exists and that they may have some exposure, but it is not directly connected to their situations. They may consider change in the future.
Concerned	"It is happening to me." Customers see the symptoms of the problem. They recognize that they are experiencing the problem and that it is potentially harmful. They are ready to define and explore the problem.
Critical	"It is costing xxx dollars." Customers have a clear picture of the problem. They are ready to quantify its financial impact."
Crisis	"I must change!" Customers recognize that the cost of the problem is unacceptable and that they can no longer avoid change. They have reached the point at which the decision to change is made."

lifting the customer to a euphoric peak with his exciting and unique solution. It is the perfect time to close and, of course, that is exactly what our salesperson attempts to do. What happens next? The customer, being asked to commit, is literally shocked out of his gaze into the utopian future and confronted with the current reality of all the risks and issues of change. Then come the objections, and the resistance to change rears its ugly head. The sales process slows down, and the sale, which the salesperson thought was "in the bag," is in serious jeopardy of being lost.

When salespeople approach the sales process from a risk and change perspective, they deal directly, and in real time, with the critical change and risk issues that their customers must resolve. Instead of selling a rosy future, they focus on helping their customers identify the consequences of staying the same or not changing the negative present. When they help customers understand the risks of staying the same and specific financial costs or lost revenues related to staying the same, the decision to buy (change) takes on a compelling urgency. They are not dealing with an optional future but with the immediate reality of a problem that they must solve. Understanding and focusing on the customer's decision to change also give the salesperson a distinct advantage and a unique position in the marketplace.

Typically, there are two processes at work in a sale: (1) the customer's buying process, which is primarily designed to obtain the best (lowest) price, and (2) the vendor's selling process, which is designed to move products and services at the best (highest) price. These processes, with their conflicting agendas, naturally generate tension and mistrust.

When we work with the customer from the perspective of a decision to change, we set aside these conflicting agendas. Now both salesperson and customer work toward a mutual objective—understanding the customer's problem and aligning the best available solution so that the customer can make the highest quality decision about the proposed change.

2. *The second focus of the most successful salespeople is on business development.* That is, successful salespeople think more like business owners than like salespeople. We call it *business think.*

Suggesting to salespeople that they need to be concerned with the development of their customers' business brings obvious agreement. "Yes, of course," they say, "we do that." But the paradigm from which most operate becomes very clear when we ask them what happens after the customer agrees to buy. The typical answers include "coordinating the installation," "getting paid," and "training the customer." The interesting thing about these responses is that they are primarily focused on what happens to the salesperson. The business being developed is the salesperson's, not the customer's.

No matter how much lip service conventional salespeople pay to developing their customer's business, they are not fooling the customer. Today's customers are forcing vendors to take an active role in their business success. Tighter supply chain management and preferred supplier programs reward sellers who help develop their customers' businesses. Those who adhere to traditional sales practices are left out in the cold. Smart professionals know that focusing on the success of the customer will ultimately improve and enrich their own business.

When we ask the best salespeople what happens after the customer agrees to buy, they say, "We help them accomplish their business objective" or "The customer will realize x dollars in reduced costs or increased revenues." The business they are developing is their customer's business.

The point is that the answers to the question need to be a balance of items that happen to the customer's business as well as items that occur in the seller's business. Seldom do we hear comments on what happens in our customer's business.

Business think means that we take the time to understand the financial, qualitative, and competitive business drivers at work in our customers' companies. It means that we frame our communication with customers in terms that they understand and that matter to them. Finally, it means that when we have delivered our solutions, we measure and evaluate success from our customers' perspective.

Business think also has profound implications for how salespeople perceive themselves. When you approach your work as a business enterprise, you quickly realize that resources are limited and must be focused to achieve their greatest potential. You know that you can't be all things to all customers and devote your energy only to the best opportunities available. You come to respect your own time and expertise as valuable resources and expect your customers to do the same.

Successful salespeople do not waste time in situations where their solutions are not required. It is also why they tend to gravitate toward the opportunities where their services are most needed and highly valued.

We describe the behavior that results from this mind-set as "going for the no." It is a mind-set that believes that at any given time, a small percentage of the marketplace will buy; therefore, we must quickly identify those that won't and set them aside for later attention. Compare this attitude to that of conventional salespeople who are taught to always be "going for the yes." They allocate their time equally among the entire universe of opportunities, and when they get in front of potential customers, they stay there until the customers disqualify them. They aren't treating their own time and expertise with respect, and it shouldn't come as much of a surprise when their customers don't either.

3. *To succeed in complex sales, the most successful salespeople are interacting with their customers by building relationships based on professionalism, trust, and cooperation.*

You could argue that all salespeople are working toward that same goal, but while that may be true in theory, it has not been translated into reality in the customer's world. In the mid-1990s, researchers asked almost 3,000 decision makers "What is the highest degree to which you trust any of the salespeople you bought from in the previous 24 months?" Only 4 percent of those surveyed said that they "completely" trusted the salespeople from whom they had bought. Nine percent said that they "substantially or generally" trusted the salesperson. Another 26 percent said they "somewhat or slightly" trusted the salesperson, and 61 percent said they trusted the salesperson "rarely or not at all."[1] Remember, these are the responses of customers about the salesperson from whom they decided to buy! What did the respondents think of the salespeople from whom they decided not to buy?

As we have already seen, this negative perception of salespeople is a problem inherent in the conventional sales process. Accordingly, the only sure way to break through the interpersonal barriers between salespeople and customers is to abandon conventional sales models. The most successful salespeople do not model typical sales behavior. The models that best reflect desired professional sales behavior are the *doctor*, the *best friend*, and the *detective*.

The Doctor

Doctors provide a model for professionalism that salespeople can relate to and emulate. Even though the medical profession today has its own image problems, let's consider it in a general sense—the medical profession at its best.

Doctors take an oath to "do no harm"; that is, do their best to leave patients in better condition than they find them. They accomplish this goal through the process of individual diagnosis. Picture a middle-age, overweight male walking into a doctor's office. Does the doctor observe the patient's appearance, note that he is a "qualified" candidate for a bypass, and recommend surgery? Of course not; it would be absurd. Doctors recognize that no medical solution is right for every patient and that they cannot diagnose patients en masse.

In contrast, salespeople regularly walk up to customers and prescribe solutions despite the fact that many of those customers may fit the profile only for the solutions in the most superficial way. The best salespeople, like doctors, diagnose each customer's condition individually and prescribe solutions that fit the unique circumstances of each case. Accordingly, their customers see them as professionals who are willing to take the time to understand their problems and can be trusted to offer solutions that not only "do no harm," but also improve the health of their businesses.

The Best Friend

When we say the best salespeople act like their customers' best friends, we don't mean that they get invited to backyard barbecues and family gatherings. Best friends are often our favorite companions, but they embody other qualities as well. Picture the most trusted person in your life—a spouse, parent, colleague, teacher, coach, or advisor. That is the relationship model we call the *best friend* model.

We expect our best friends to look out for our best interests. They help to protect us from errors in judgment. We also look to our best friends for honest opinions and answers. We trust them to tell us the truth. The best salespeople use the role of best friend as a litmus test. They ask themselves, "If this customer were my best friend, what would I advise in this situation?" When it comes time to offer solutions, they ask, "Is this the answer I would propose if this customer were my best friend? Do I have his best interests in mind or my own?"

The Detective

The third role that successful salespeople model is one of personal style and interpersonal process. In a television series, actor Peter Falk convincingly played Detective Columbo—an unusual kind of detective. He never threatened a suspect. In fact, he rarely even raised his voice. Columbo was mild-mannered and nonthreatening to the point of appearing ineffective. In fact, the show's criminals consistently underestimated this detective—at least in the early stages of the investigation. It was a natural mistake. Columbo made them feel safe and secure, and while they congratulated themselves on their craftiness, the detective quietly went about the business of diagnosing the situation and reconstructing the crime.

Amazingly, Columbo solved every crime he ever investigated (television series aren't exactly real life scenarios). He accomplished this feat in two ways: by observing the most minute details of the crime scene and by asking a seemingly endless number of polite, unassuming questions. By the way, Columbo's methods provide an excellent contrast to James Bond's. Bond, whom we examined in the last chapter, already knows all the answers, so he doesn't need to ask any questions. All that he needs to do is verbally challenge and strong-arm the villain.

As salespeople, we need to emulate the detective. We need to fully understand what is happening in our customer's world. We can accomplish this goal in the same nonconfrontational way that Columbo solved crimes, through the power of observation and the process of questioning and clarifying the things that we see. In *The Trusted Advisor* (Free Press, 2000), David Maister devotes a full chapter to the effectiveness of the Columbo model. He also notes, the main barrier to using this effective model is our own emotional need to be the center of attention.

A Set of Skills for Complex Sales

The second element of any profession encompasses the skills and tools that its practitioners use to achieve their goals. Skills, as defined earlier, are the mental and physical ability to manipulate the tools that professionals use to execute systems.

In a complex sales process, the most successful salespeople are capable of using a large number of tools. Most of these are specific to certain elements of the sales process, and we discuss them in later chapters. Three major tools span the entire selling process and, as such, are best introduced before we describe the process itself.

These three tools help us answer one of the basic questions present in every complex sale: *Who* should be involved in decisions determining the problem, the design, and the implementation of the solution? *What* are the problems that the customer is actually experiencing? *How* are those problems impeding the customers' ability to accomplish their business objectives? *How* are those problems connected to the salesperson's solutions? *How* will successful business outcomes be achieved for the customer? The answers to these questions represent an equation we need to solve to successfully navigate a complex sale:

> Right People + Right Questions + Right Sequence = Quality Decisions

Right People—The Cast of Characters

It follows that if customers do not have a quality decision process, it is not likely they would assemble the best group of people to be involved in the decision. In the complex decision, the search for the elusive, single decision maker is futile. There is always the individual who can say no, even if everyone else says yes, and that same individual can say yes when everyone else is saying no. Reality shows that today's complex decisions are far more likely to evolve from a group initiative and consensus. Smart business executives realize that successful implementation is directly related to the degree of buy-in. This fact does not alleviate the need to find decision makers; it actually raises that task to a more sophisticated level.

One telling observation from the field is that when it comes to identifying and interacting with decision makers in a complex sale, the most successful salespeople don't take the hand that is dealt them. They don't accept the decision makers identified by their customers without question. Rather, they understand that customers who do not have a quality decision process in place are unlikely to be able to assemble an effective and efficient decision-making team. As a result, successful sales professionals take an active role in building the optimal "cast" for their customers. They seek to identify the important cast members in the customer's organization, involve each in the decision process, and ensure that each has all the assistance required to comprehend the problem, the opportunity, and the solution. Effectively managing the decision team is a job that spans the entire complex sales process. We call the tool used to achieve that task the *cast of characters*, and it helps us identify and access the right people.

The key to casting a complex sale is *perspective*. The cast of a complex sale needs to include a set of players that encompasses each of the perspectives required in a quality decision. In every sale, there are two major perspectives: The *problem perspective* includes members of the customer's organization who can help identify, understand, and communicate the details and cost of the problem. The *solution perspective* includes those who can help identify, understand, and communicate the appropriate design, investment, and measurement criteria of the solution.

Casting doesn't stop here. We also need decision team members who can bring the perspectives available at different levels of the organization to the table. For both the problem and the solution perspectives, we need to include individuals, internal and external, who represent and/or advise the executive, managerial, and operational levels of the customer's organization.

Why go through all this work? The obvious answer is that there is no other way to ensure that you are developing all of the information needed to guide your customer to a high-quality decision. There are also some less obvious answers. For instance, would you prefer to present a solution to a group that has had little or no input into its content, or would you rather present a solution proposal to a group that has already taken an active role in creating it? Would you prefer to deal with a newly installed decision maker who has replaced your single contact in the middle of the sales process, or would you rather face that new decision maker with the support of all the remaining cast members and with full documentation of the progress already made?

The answers to these questions are clear. The successful sales professional casts the complex sale to assemble the group of players who has the most impact, information, insight, and influence on the decision to buy. This shortens the sales cycle by effectively reaching the right people and helping them make high-quality decisions. You build predictability into your sales results and ultimately shorten the sales cycle time.

Right Questions—Diagnostic Questions

All salespeople are taught to use questions in the sales process, but most use questions in ineffective ways and in dubious pursuits. They ask questions to get their customers to volunteer information they have been taught is critical to the sale. Their goal is to identify who makes the decision to buy and to determine how much the customer is willing to spend on a solution. They want to maximize their contact with customers and get customers to pinpoint their own problems. All of these reasons subvert the most valuable use of questions—to diagnose.

The most successful salespeople are sophisticated diagnosticians. They understand that to effectively and accurately diagnose a customer's situation, they must be able to create a conversational flow designed to ask the right people the right questions. They also know that they gain more credibility through the questions they ask their customers than anything they can ever tell them.

The "right questions" refers to four types of *diagnostic questions* that salespeople use to understand and communicate customers' problems:

1. *A to Z* questions frame a customer process and then ask customers to pinpoint specific areas of concern within it.

2. *Indicator* questions uncover observable symptoms of problems.

3. *Assumptive* questions expand the customer's comprehension of the problem in nonthreatening ways.

4. *Rule of Two* questions help identify preferred alternatives or respond to negative issues by giving the customer permission to be honest, without fear of retribution from the salesperson.

These diagnostic questions, which we detail in chapters that follow, are purposely designed to avoid turning conversations into interrogations, or rote interviews and surveys. Instead, they help salespeople develop integrated conversations, in which the customer's self-esteem is protected, mutual value is generated, and communication is stimulated. (Silence and listening skills, as we describe later, also play important ancillary roles in diagnostic questioning.)

Right Sequence—The Bridge to Change

Just as complex sales feature multiple decision makers, they also require multiple decisions. The content and sequencing of those decisions is what allows us to connect our customers and the problems they face to the solutions that we are offering. To accomplish this goal, we need to establish an ordered, repeatable sequence of questions that will lead to a high-quality decision.

This sequence is called the *bridge to change* and is patterned after the methods physicians are taught to diagnose complex medical conditions and prescribe appropriate solutions (see Figure 3.2). It guides salespeople by establishing a questioning flow capable of leading their customers through complex decisions. More importantly, it allows salespeople to pinpoint the areas in which they can construct value connections that will benefit their customers.

The bridge has nine main links; each is a potential area for creating and capturing value. It starts at the organizational level by examining the customer's major business objectives or drivers and the critical success factors (CSFs) that must be attained to achieve those objectives. It seeks to identify the individuals responsible for each CSF and to understand their personal performance objectives. The bridge prompts the salesperson to identify performance gaps by

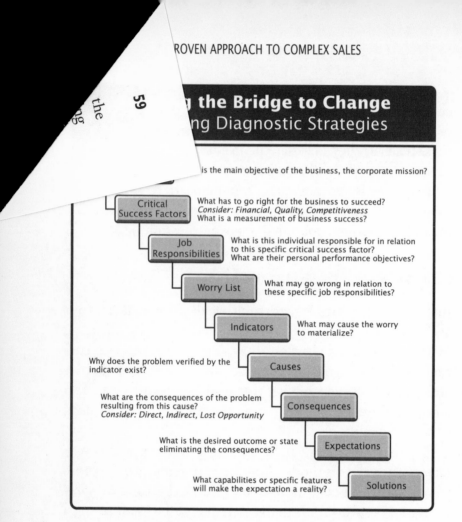

FIGURE 3.2 Building the Bridge to Change—
Developing Diagnostic Strategies

identifying potential shortfalls in the customer's key performance indicators, probing for their symptoms, uncovering their causes, and quantifying their consequences. In its last links, the bridge helps define the expectations and alternatives for solving the customer's problems and then narrows the search to a final solution.

The bridge to change functions like a decision tree. Each branch of the tree is integral to a quality decision. Each link logically connects to the next, and although we can travel several branches simultaneously, none can be skipped without disrupting the decision process and, of course, the potential sale. In fact, when you hear customer objections, what you are actually hearing is the direct result of a skipped or less-than-fully traveled branch. If each branch has been completed to a customer's satisfaction, all of their potential objections have, by definition, already been resolved. The customer can, of course, still refuse to buy, but it is unlikely that their refusal will be based on any reason within the salesperson's control.

The three tools—cast of characters, diagnostic questions, and the bridge to change—and the ability to consistently use them, represent the key skills of a diagnostic sales professional. They also represent the three components of the complex sales equation—right people, right questions, and right sequence.

A System for Complex Sales

The final element in the foundation of a profession is its system. A *system*, in this broad sense, is an organized process and set procedures that lead to a predictable result. Our system is based on our observations of successful sales professionals and is called the *Diagnostic Business Development*® process, which is often referred to as the *prime process*.

Diagnostic Business Development offers us a platform on which to understand and integrate our professional skills. This represents a quantum leap beyond typical sales training, which is usually skill-based and which leaves salespeople with a briefcase full of tools, but no systematic way to apply them to achieve their ultimate goal.

Diagnostic Business Development is a metaprocess, one that can be overlaid on any complex sale. It provides a navigable path from the first step of identifying potential customers, through the sale itself and onto expanding and retaining profitable customer relationships. It is a system that encompasses all of the critical activities of the sales professional and provides the decision-making assistance that customers involved in a complex business decision so desperately need.

As we see in Chapter 9, it is also an extended process that ranges from product inception to customer consumption. It can be used to enhance the communication and integration between major business functions, from product development to marketing, to sales, service, and support.

Because Diagnostic Business Development covers the entire profession of complex selling, it naturally encompasses a great deal of information. To facilitate comprehension and ease of use, we divided the process into four subsystems or phases. The phases of the process are related in a linear fashion and are organized by the major activity that is undertaken in each specific phase. They are *Discover*, *Diagnose*, *Design*, and *Deliver* (see Figure 3.3).

Discover

Discover is about research and preparation. It encompasses how salespeople get ready to engage and serve customers. Everyone who sells starts at the same point—the identification of a customer. In conventional sales, this is called *prospecting and qualification*, which, unfortunately, is often characterized by minimal preparation. In Discover, however, we expand the preparation into a process, which is aimed at the identification of a specific customer who has the highest probability of change.

Discover means pushing beyond the traditional boundaries of prospecting to create a solid foundation on which to build a long-term, profitable relationship. It

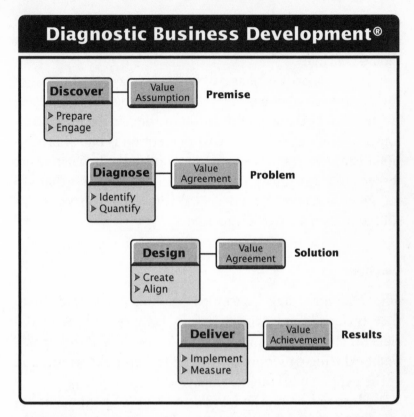

FIGURE 3.3 Integrated Diagnostic Business Development®

recognizes the fact that *every qualified prospect will not become a customer*. It embraces that realization by actively looking for reasons to disqualify a prospect and by refusing to unnecessarily waste the time and resources of the prospect or the sales professional.

The tasks in the Discover process include precontact research of potential customers and their industry. Discover also includes the preparation of an engagement strategy, which includes an introduction, some basic assumptions about the value that could be created, and a conversational bridge designed for that specific customer. In addition, it includes the initial contact with the prospective customer, during which this information is communicated. Customer and salesperson mutually decide whether the sales process should continue.

In the Discover phase, as in each succeeding phase of the Diagnostic Business Development process, salespeople are actively building a perception of themselves in the customer's mind. In this case, that perception is one of professionalism. We want customers to understand that mutual respect and trust govern our relationship. We want them to see us as competent, well versed in their business, and a source of competitive advantage.

Diagnose

The Diagnose stage encompasses how salespeople help their prospects and customers fully comprehend the inefficiencies and performance gaps. It is a process of *hyperqualification* during which we pursue an in-depth determination of the extent and financial impact of their problems.

Most selling methodologies recognize the importance of understanding customers' problems and, accordingly, often tack some form of needs analysis onto their process. However, the true intention of needs analysis is usually subverted. First, we find that it is used to get the customer to make observations and reach conclusions. In essence, customers are asked to diagnose themselves: What are your issues and what are you looking for? Second, the questions salespeople ask their customers are more often about the customer's buying process than their situation: What are you looking for, who will make the decision, when will you make the decision, how much do you want to spend? Finally, and in the worst cases, needs analysis is used as a highly biased review to justify the salesperson's solutions.

With Diagnostic Business Development, diagnosis is not subordinate to solutions or the sale. It is meant to maximize customers' objective awareness of their dissatisfaction, whether that dissatisfaction supports the salesperson's offerings or not.

In the Diagnose phase, the process most radically diverges from conventional selling. Our research tells us that during a well-executed diagnostic process, the customer makes the decision to buy and from whom to buy. In the more traditional approach, salespeople are looking for this decision after the presentation and during "the close." Therefore, in the Diagnose phase, the most critical elements of the complex sale occur.

The salesperson's tasks during the Diagnose phase begin when we shift the emphasis of our fact finding to focusing on the customer's internal issues. At this point, we need to deepen our understanding of our customers' business, their job responsibilities, perspectives, and concerns. Diagnosis also includes measuring the assumptions about customers' problems that we presented in the Discover phase against the reality of the situation and quantifying the actual cost of the problem. It includes a collaborative effort to evolve a comprehensive view of the problem to customers, thus allowing them to make an informed decision as to whether they need to change.

In the Diagnose phase, we want our customers to perceive us as credible. We establish our credibility by our ability to identify, evaluate, and communicate the sources and intensity of their problems, as well as helping them recognize opportunities they are not aware of. We reinforce that credibility by refusing to alter the customer's reality to fit our own needs.

Design

Design encompasses how salespeople help the customer create and understand the solution. It is a collaborative and highly interactive effort to help customers sort through their expectations and alternatives to arrive at an optimal solution.

In a more conventional sales approach, design equals presentation, and, in presentation, the customer is not involved in the design of the solution. As a result, they do not develop a significant degree of ownership of that solution. The conventional salesperson may say, "This is the product we offer that is best suited to your situation." Then they proceed to reel off a litany of features and technical information specific to that solution.

In the Diagnostic Business Development process, however, the Design phase is not focused on a specific solution. Its goal is to get salespeople and customers working together to identify the optimal solution to the problems that were uncovered and quantified in the Diagnose phase.

There is an important distinction here. An optimal solution does not mean the product or service that we are charged with selling right now is best suited to the customer's problem. *Rather, the optimal solution is a series of product or service parameters that minimizes the customer's risk of change and optimizes return on investment.* By staying true to the objective of a quality business decision, where that solution will be found is a secondary consideration at this stage in the decision process.

The tasks included in the Design phase are aimed at establishing and understanding the decision criteria the customer will use to find a solution to the problem. This aim requires us to establish the solution results the customer would expect, the quantifiable business values for those outcomes (and thus, the available funding for the acquisition of the solution), and the timing in which it must be delivered. We manage customer expectations during the Design process by introducing and exploring alternatives, including solutions offered by competitors. We also teach customers the questions they should be asking of all potential suppliers to assure their quality decision.

In the Design phase, we want our customers to perceive a high degree of integrity in all our behaviors. We establish our integrity by creating a solution framework that best solves their problems. It frames a set of decision criteria that we would use to determine what to select for ourselves or would recommend without hesitating, if our best friends were experiencing this particular problem. The conclusion of the Design phase is what we call a *discussion document*. This document provides a summary of the diagnosis with a "pencil sketch" of the solution. It is used to do a final sanity check before completing a formal proposal and presentation. It is the dress rehearsal, your final run through, and it assures there will be no surprises during the final presentation.

Deliver

In the final phase of the Diagnostic Business Development process, the work of the previous phases comes to fruition. It encompasses how the salesperson assures the customer's success in executing the solution.

While the conventional sales process forces salespeople to overcome objections and try to close the sale, the diagnostic approach allows customers to evolve their own decisions. Customers who have traveled through the Diagnostic Business Development process have a clear understanding of their problems, and they know what the best solution will look like. In fact, they are coauthors of that solution. *Salespeople who use the Diagnostic Business Development process and have not disqualified the customer by this point in the process experience exceptional conversion ratios.* That is why we say that the ultimate goal in the Deliver phase is to maximize the customer's awareness of the value derived from the solution that is being implemented.

The tasks in the Deliver phase begin with the preparation and presentation of a formal proposal and the customer's official acceptance of the solution. The next steps include the delivery and support of the solution and the measurement and evaluation of the results that have been delivered. The final task of the Deliver phase is the maintenance and growth of our relationship with the customer.

In the Deliver phase, we want our customers to perceive us as dependable. We literally do what we said we were going to do. As we complete the sale, our customers should be thinking: You are there for me; you will take care of me; I can depend on you.

The four phases of the Diagnostic Business Development process—the Prime Process—represent a reengineering of the conventional sales process. The process eliminates the inherent flaws in conventional sales processes and directly addresses the challenges that salespeople face while trying to master complex sales in today's marketplace.

Creating Value through Diagnostic Business Development

Value is a critical concept that no salesperson can afford to ignore. *Value* can be defined as incremental results the customer is willing to pay for. To successfully complete a sale, salespeople know that they must be able to create value for their customers and they must be able to capture a reasonable share of that value for their company.

Most salespeople are unable to manage the challenge of creating and capturing value for two reasons:

1. The increasing commoditization of their offerings renders their ability to communicate that value to customers ineffective.

2. The increasing complexity of problems and solutions makes it ever more difficult for customers to comprehend the true value of their solutions when that value is present.

Even when their managers instruct them to create and capture value, they are rarely told how to accomplish this feat. As a result, value creation is more of a buzzword than a tangible reality.

The Prime Process offers a two-part answer to that dilemma. First, it is a unique value-based process that is connected to value in a lock-step progression. Thus, as you complete each of the four phases of the Prime Process, your customer is one step further along the path to attaining value.

We all approach our work from a *value proposition* established in our companies. These propositions, which are usually stated in the most general terms, define the markets addressed by our solutions and identify the potential value our solutions offer that group of customers. The guidance provided by value propositions gives us a platform from which we can undertake the Discover phase of the Prime Process.

In discovery, we identify a prospective customer and refine our value proposition in the specific terms of that customer's likely business situation, problems, and objectives. We literally tailor the value proposition so it fits a single customer. We call this version of the value proposition a *value assumption* (see Figure 3.4). The value assumption is a hypothesis as to the value we believe we could bring to this specific customer. The key point is

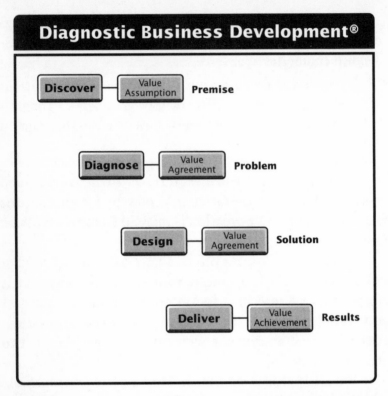

FIGURE 3.4 Integrated Diagnostic Business Development®

we are not making a boastful claim; we are discussing possibilities.

In turn, a value assumption becomes the premise for the diagnosis. In the Diagnose phase, we further develop and test the assumptions we have made about the definition and scope of the customer's situation. We determine to what degree our assumptions are correct; that is, the symptoms and indicators are occurring in the customer's business. We identify and quantify the impact of the absence of our value. To the degree the assumptions are correct and the customer agrees with us, we have the beginnings of *value agreement with the customer on the dimensions of the problem.*

We continue the evolution of the value agreement during the Design phase. The objective of the Design phase is to collaborate with the customer to create a solution that is aligned with the issues and expectations of the customer. The outcome of the Design phase is a *value agreement with the customer on the dimensions of the value our solution* will bring to the customer.

With a complete value agreement defined, we can move to the final step of the Diagnostic Business Development process—Deliver. In the Deliver phase, we implement the solution and measure results. Delivering value to the customer is the ultimate and highest goal of salespeople: *value achievement* for our customers and ourselves. The integrated Diagnostic Business Development process is shown in Figure 3.3.

Second, the Prime Process enables sales professionals to leverage the value they deliver to customers at three levels. In ascending order of complexity, profitable return, and competitive advantage, these are the Product, Process, and Performance levels of value.

At the Product level, the value focus is on the product or service itself. Product quality, availability, and cost are the major sources of value at this level. Typically, the salesperson is dealing with purchasing and competing with like products and services.

Conventional sales strategies are limited to the leverage of value at the Product level. They make only the most tenuous connection with the customer. Thus, in their customers' eyes, this is a commodity sale, subject to the price pressures we have already described.

At the Process level, the delivery of value is expanded from the product (or service) being sold to the process in which the customer will use it. The optimization of the process becomes the major source of value at this level. Typically, the salesperson and his team are working with operating managers in the various departments at a tactical level. The sale itself becomes an integral part of a process improvement effort.

At the Process level of value, sales professionals are creating a limited partnership with the customer. In their customers' eyes, this sale delivers a greater degree of value than a commodity-based transaction, but the relationship has shallow roots. It can easily lose its value for the customer when the process is optimized or if the process becomes outmoded or is eliminated.

The Performance level offers the greatest potential for value leverage and it is the highest value level which a sales professional can achieve. The development of the customer's business becomes the major source of value at this level. Typically, the sales professional is working with senior executives, as well as the operations level, and the sale is

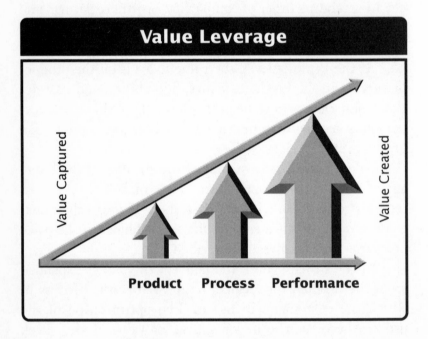

FIGURE 3.5 Value Leverage

only one manifestation of an ongoing relationship that is connected to the organization at an enterprise level.

Prime Process sales professionals are creating and capturing the optimal value at the Product and Process levels; their ultimate objective is to reach the Performance level. At this level, they create strategic partnerships with their customers. In their customers' eyes, the sale is an investment in a more profitable future and the relationship with the seller is a valuable asset. Relationships like this are not easily uprooted. (The relationship among the three levels of value is shown in Figure 3.5.)

In terms of value leverage, it is important to note that we define customers in a broad sense that includes all sales channels. For instance, if you are delivering products and services through a distribution network or channel partners, you should be considering how to enhance each of their businesses, as well as your end-users' businesses, at the Product, Process, and Performance levels.

In this chapter, we introduced the systems, skills, and disciplines behind mastering the complex sale. In the next four chapters, we show each phase of the Diagnostic Business Development process in greater detail to help you better understand how the major elements of the complex sale operate in practice and to help you get the results you are looking for.

4

Discover the Prime Customer

Optimum Engagement Strategies

In the *Discover* phase of the Diagnostic Business Development process, we establish a profile of the ideal customer for our offerings, match that profile to customers on an individualized basis, and craft a customized engagement strategy for initial contact. Its goal is to identify those customers who are most likely to be experiencing the issues our offerings address and the absence of the value we provide and, therefore, who have the highest probability of buying our products and services. The Discover phase encompasses all of the preparation activity before the actual diagnosis.

Discover is an especially critical element in complex sales. As the complexity and uniqueness of customers increase, so, too, does the need for and return on preparation. The greater our ability to customize and personalize our engagement strategies for individual customers, the greater our chances are of successfully gaining entry to their organizations and the more likely they are to feel that offerings have been designed specifically for them and that we are speaking directly to their world and their responsibilities.

Unfortunately, in their zeal to get face to face with customers, too many salespeople put far too little time and effort into this work. The percentage of salespeople who continue to "wing it" as they approach high-level executives is appalling. The typical attitude toward preparation all too often runs along these lines: If it walks like a duck and it quacks like a duck, a good salesperson should be able to sell anything made for ducks or, for that matter, anything made for birds. Therefore, the attitude, "Why prepare?" The problem in complex sales is that this one-size-fits-all attitude toward customers has worn out its welcome; it just won't fly. Nor should it.

Customers resist being treated as generic candidates for good reasons. First, they realize that they are simply impersonal targets in the eyes of the salesperson. They rightly suspect that they will be subjected to a one-sided view of the world and, perhaps, high pressure and other sales manipulations. Further, because their unique characteristics, situations, and problems have been largely ignored in the past, there is little basis for believing that the products and services being offered will create the optimal value for them. They believe that the time they spend with the salesperson may ultimately bring little, if any, return.

Just as significant is the fact that salespeople should also be avoiding the generic treatment of customers. The commonly accepted idea is that to maximize their performance, salespeople must maximize the number of prospects they see and the number of proposals they present. Thus, the less time they spend in preparation equates to more prospects and, somehow, increased sales, but it clearly doesn't work that way. Spending time with customers you aren't prepared for and who are unlikely to buy is inefficient and ineffective.

If you want to maximize sales results, you cannot simply allocate your time equally among all potential customers in your market. Instead, you must concentrate on the customer who has the highest probability of being negatively impacted by the absence of your solution and, therefore, the corresponding high probability of being receptive to your solution. The identification of that customer and the preparation to engage that customer is the purpose of Discover. If you rush through it unprepared, you end up gambling your time and efforts on an unknown prospect and, as a result, substantially lower your ability to predict your chances of success in the complex sale.

Key Thought
Is There Someplace Better I Could Be?

We keep the idea of the Prime customer in the front of our minds by continually asking ourselves a simple, but fundamentally radical, question: *Is there someplace better I could be?* Successful salespeople understand that the best place to be is the place where they can leverage their efforts and maximize their overall performance as well as their customer's. They are continually moving toward that optimal engagement. As elements of success decrease with a current customer, at a certain point, the odds of success become greater with a new customer. There is someplace better we can be, and we need to take ourselves and our resources elsewhere.

How do sales professionals identify the best opportunities? Through a more comprehensive and creative approach to the Discover process, an approach designed to help salespeople:

- Develop a clear understanding of the market for their offerings.
- Identify and understand their potential customers.
- Design the most effective engagement strategy for an individual customer.
- Conduct the initial contact in a way that encourages the customer to invite them in and provide access to information and people.
- Establish a diagnostic agreement that sets the stage for the next phase of the Prime Process.

Goals of the Discover phase can be divided into two groups: those that salespeople undertake to prepare for the initial engagement and execution of the engagement itself. We now take a closer look at these goals, how they are achieved, and how they add up to successfully complete the work of Discover.

Understanding Your Value

Every salesperson should consider this ancient proverb before embarking on the complex sale: "Know thyself."[1] It means that before we start trying to understand our customers' worlds, we should develop a full understanding of our own world and have a guiding vision that begins to define the ideal customer. More specifically, we need to understand our offerings, the markets they target, and the quantitative and qualitative levels of activity we must attain to reach our personal performance goals.

Self-knowledge begins with the *value proposition* inherent in the goods and services we are offering customers. In the context of complex sales, when we discuss value propositions, we are talking about the positive business and personal impact that your offerings deliver to your customers. This value represents your competitive advantage in the marketplace. It also forms a baseline from which you can begin to measure the fit between your offerings and prospective customers. The unique characteristics of your offerings help you define the ideal customer. If you are selling a logistics software package that allows the user to manage and coordinate tens of thousands of small packages with different destinations, the best place to spend your time is not with a company whose shipping patterns indicate that it transports full containers to only a limited number of destinations.

Obviously, this customer will not be able to receive the value available in your solutions.

The analysis of the value proposition yields valuable conclusions about the characteristics of the most qualified customers for our offerings. For instance, if our company is a leader in innovative solutions, we should be looking for the early adopters in our target markets. If we are the high-value supplier in our industry, we should be looking for the customers who are the high-value suppliers in their respective markets. Value propositions tell us what segment of the industry is most likely to buy, what size company we should contact, and who we should seek out inside those companies. This information allows us to begin constructing an external and internal profile of what our ideal customer looks like.

This is common sense, but it is surprising how often we have found companies changing their value propositions without integrating those changes into the way the salesforce operates, how often changes in the selling environment render an existing value proposition ineffective, and/or how often we find salespeople who simply don't understand the value proposition they are offering.

Once you understand the value proposition you are offering customers, you can create a *personal business development plan*. An effective personal business plan must be linked to overall corporate strategy and operational objectives. We are all members of corporate teams, and our goals must be contributory to those of the larger organizational goals.

A personal business plan must have both quantitative and qualitative components. Most salespeople are already familiar with the quantitative aspect of a business plan. It is the common approach that tells us that if we contact a predetermined number of prospective customers, we will set a fixed number of appointments, that x number of appointments results in y number of presentations, and that y number of presentations yields z number of sales. The problem is that most plans stop right there, and salespeople end up struggling to achieve their quotas by crunching through vast numbers of prospects, working harder—not smarter.

Sales-by-numbers advocates do make sales, but they never excel at the complex sale and certainly are not making the best use of their resources. What they are missing is the qualitative element of the personal business plan. Qualitative metrics, which we have already derived from the value proposition, add an important dimension to a personal business plan. They allow us to begin to optimize our efforts and resources. For example, instead of simply telling us that we must call on 12 companies, a qualitative measure might take into account the fact that our value proposition is most attractive to companies with revenues between $15 million and $50 million and is more heavily weighted toward the top end of that range. Accordingly, our plan might stipulate that one-third of the companies we call on have annual revenues between $15 million and $30 million, that two-thirds have revenues between $31 million and $50 million, and that we do not call on companies whose revenues are above or below those figures.

The final component in understanding our own world is the *opportunity management system* that enables us to organize and schedule the activities of the personal business plan and the ensuing interaction with customers. There is only the most superficial need for opportunity management in conventional sales—the traditional salesperson chooses a prospective customer and drives that customer as far through the selling process as possible. Then, the salesperson moves on to the next opportunity.

In the Prime Process methodology, opportunity management is a more fluid process. Every customer is treated with a determined level of priority. Some prospective customers do not fit your qualification criteria at the time you first look at them; therefore, they may be monitored only at regular intervals to see if their fundamental indicators have changed. Others show a strong initial fit and are scheduled for further research.

Opportunity management encompasses how we develop and manage our leads. It includes early warning systems that tell us when specific customers are optimal for contact. For instance, a salesperson providing office storage systems might track commercial building permits and commercial real estate to identify sales leads. A building permit equates to a new building, which equates to new storage requirements.

As the opportunity represented by each customer changes, so does their priority in the salesperson's schedule. The ultimate purpose of opportunity management is to point salespeople toward that single individual or company that represents the best place they could be at any particular moment.

Pinpointing the Prime Customer

Once we understand what an ideal customer should look like, the work of the Discover stage shifts to the individual customer. Successful salespeople take the time to prepare for the initial conversation with potential customers. They construct external and internal profiles of the customer's organization and ensure that those profiles match the profile of the ideal customer. They identify the driving forces and perspectives at work in the customer's organization and become familiar with the customer's goals.

By completing this work, sales professionals lay the groundwork for a successful initial conversation. They create a basis for engagement that enables them to speak with customers using the customer's language, frame the initial conversation around issues of importance to their customers, and build a perception of professionalism in the customers' minds that clearly differentiates them from their competition.

An external customer portrait tells us what customers look like from the outside, their demographics. It includes information such as the physical details of the company (size, revenues), industry and market position, and key characteristics that differentiate it from its competitors. An internal profile has two dimensions: how companies and the individuals within them think—which we call their *psychographics*—and what they are experiencing, their current situation. What are the indicators and symptoms that would manifest in the absence of the value you can provide? Psychographics includes information about how its leaders and employees approach and perceive their world—the organization's strategies, its driving forces and goals, and the

---

Key Thought
When Working with Limited Resources in a Highly Competitive Environment, the Accuracy of Your Aim Is Crucial

In the complex sale, we are dealing with organizations where access is constantly sought and is tightly controlled. It is difficult to reach into the cast of characters; if we do engage, there is precious little time to differentiate and establish our value. Developing a full understanding of the customer before we make formal contact maximizes our chances of achieving a constructive engagement and developing the level of access required to accomplish our goals.

attitudes and beliefs that underpin the behavior and decision making of management. The situational profile points out the physical conditions that, when present, will likely drive a decision to change.

There are myriad resources that a salesperson can tap into for the previous information. The customer's annual reports, Web sites, publications of all sorts, and existing vendors of noncompetitive products; the salesperson's industry contacts and current customers in the same industry; employees in the potential customer's organization . . . the list goes on and on. More important, and less common than a recitation of sources for customer information, is the content and analysis of the data we collect. Visit our Web site at www.primeresource.com for valuable links to popular information resources.

One effective way to analyze an organization is in terms of its business drivers, critical success factors or business objectives (see Figure 4.1). It is important to be able to categorize your offerings to effectively align your capabilities to your client's objectives. To simplify what could become an overwhelming list, we have determined that all business objectives can be placed neatly into one of three major categories:

1. *Financial drivers* are manifested by goals specifying either top-line growth via increased revenues or bottom-line growth via reduced expenses.
2. *Quality drivers* are manifested by goals based on increasing the satisfaction of the organization's customers, employees, or, for those in heavily regulated industries, regulators.
3. *Competitive drivers* are manifested by goals related to making offerings unique and assuring the availability of products or services to customers.

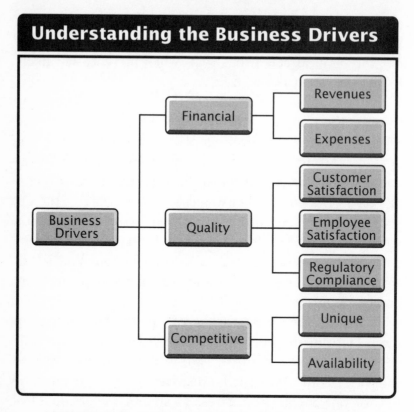

FIGURE 4.1   Understanding the Business Drivers

To identify long-term drivers, look to the customer's Web site for mission and vision statements. For short-term drivers, read the CEO's message in the annual report. It is a rare message that does not include concrete statements about the critical success factors driving the business currently and what will drive it in the near future. Confirm that the drivers identified in these sources are current (they can change fast) and then ask: To what degree are they at work in your prospective customer's business? How do they connect to your offerings?

What about the corporate culture at work in a customer's company? Personality and values trickle down from the top, so the smart profiler pays particular attention to the customer's executive committee members. What are their backgrounds? CEOs and other leaders who have risen to power have come out of different functions and, accordingly, have different perspectives. A CEO with a sales background may be focused on customer satisfaction; one with an engineering background may be more focused more on innovation. This information is often found in the public domain and is readily available.

The recent history of an organization also yields valuable clues to the atmosphere and personalities you can expect to encounter when you contact customers. Have there been restructuring, workforce reductions, mergers, and acquisitions? All of these events leave a mark on the organization and offer clues as to what objectives and emotions drive their decision-making criteria.

We close this discussion with an example of creative customer profiling at the Discover stage. A major player in the trucking industry was initiating a complete logistics management service. Its customer profile called for a manufacturer who was a forward-thinking innovator in other business processes. The team set its sights on earning the business of a major computer manufacturer. One way in which the sales team developed its understanding of the potential customer was to spend several days outside the company's manufacturing facilities. They counted the number of trucks inbound and outbound and the number of different trucking companies represented. The team talked to drivers at local truck stops to get a sense of the size of the loads, their origins, and final destinations. They used the raw data they collected to create a picture of the computer maker's logistics flow and calculate estimates of the related costs. When the sales team finally met with the computer manufacturer's management, the managers were astounded by the sales team's depth of knowledge about

---

Key Thought
Credibility

Expected credibility is what you know about your solution and your business. Exceptional credibility is what you know about your customer and their business.

---

their operation and intrigued by the potential value that could be achieved through the company's logistics services. They elected to pursue the matter further and eventually transferred their logistics business to our client.

The point here is not that we should start camping out at our customer's facilities. Instead, it is that the better developed our profile of a potential customer is before we initiate contact, the greater our ability to create a strong value assumption; there are endless means of acquiring intelligence before the initial engagement. This, in turn, enables us to craft a one-of-a-kind introduction, one that our customers will feel was prepared specifically for them and could not be used with anyone else. It allows us to quickly hone in on the customer's critical issues, establish ourselves as professionals, and differentiate ourselves from the competition. In short, it represents extreme relevancy. This creates a compelling platform for a very constructive engagement and immediate and complete access to the customer.

Diagnostic Positioning—Creating the Engagement Strategy

When the external and internal profiles we develop confirm our view of a prospective customer as a Prime customer, it is time to create an engagement strategy for our initial contact.

> ### Key Thought
> ### In the Eyes of Customers, Salespeople
> ### Are Guilty until Proven Innocent
>
> This may sound harsh, but it is nonetheless a reality that sales professionals must be prepared to face. The most effective way to break through a customer's preconceived notions about salespeople is to do something actors call "playing against type." When we act in unfamiliar ways, customers are jarred into seeing beyond the stereotypical character they have come to expect.

There are two elements in an engagement strategy: One is unchanging and comprises the framework on which we will always structure our encounters with customers; the second is ever-changing and is the identification of the best entry point into the customer's organization.

Breaking Type

There are several ways that successful salespeople play against type. We've already introduced the first in Chapter 3—*going for the no*—the idea that as salespeople, we should always and actively be looking for reasons to end engagements with individuals we can't help. When we are willing to break off or suspend an engagement with a customer who is not experiencing a problem that our offering can solve, we play against the stereotype that says salespeople never take no for an answer.

An extension of the concept of *going for the no* and another way we can play against type is to *always be leaving*. How do most salespeople appear to the customer, relative to "staying" or "leaving?" That's right—they look like furniture—they're not likely to leave, like a pesky little pit bull clamped on your ankle. The more you try to shake it off, the tighter those little jaws clamp down. To be rid of the stereotypical salesperson, customers expect to have to hang up the phone mid-sentence or call in security. Salespeople who are unwilling to end engagements leave their customers feeling pressured and tense. But when we indicate our willingness to step back, customers feel free to communicate openly and without fear that the information they share will be used against them.

We can communicate these attitudes from the very beginning of our contact with customers. For example, on our first phone call with a potential customer, we can introduce ourselves and then, as a prelude to the subject of the call, say, "I'm not sure if it is appropriate that we should be talking . . ." That simple phrase relaxes the customer and indicates that the salesperson is not about to force his or her way forward. It tells the customer that the salesperson is willing to be somewhere else if that is more appropriate. It clearly sets the stage for a professional encounter.

One last way we can play against type is by *being prepared not to be prepared*. The stereotypical salesperson feels pressured to always have an answer. Part of the reason lies in human nature itself; no one likes to admit that they don't know the answer to a question. The other part is that a conventional salesperson sees a customer's question as a golden opportunity to start presenting. Prime salespeople, however, break type. Because they are completely prepared, they can afford to be relaxed and casual. They don't need to force an answer before they fully understand the customer's situation and, as important, they understand that even when they do have an answer, if the customer is not prepared to hear it or won't fully understand it, it might not be the right time to offer it.

For instance, customers often ask salespeople, "What makes your product better than your competitor's?" The natural response is to launch into a dissertation about the unique benefits of your offering, and when you do, you are fulfilling the image of the conventional salesperson. The counterintuitive response is to step back from the challenge and say, "I'm not sure that it is. Our competitor makes a fine product and at this point, I don't understand enough about your situation to recommend which product may be a better fit for your application. Let me ask you this . . ." and then goes on to ask the next diagnostic question. The salesperson who responds in this manner opens the door to a more in-depth discussion and greater involvement. The key to the engagement strategy is the *diagnostic positioning*—we are positioned to Diagnose, not present.

Identifying the Optimum Point of Entry

The final element of the precontact phase of Discover is the identification of the best point of entry into the customer's organization. In conventional sales, the point of entry is usually fixed by the job title of the contact and frequently targets "the buyer." Sellers of training programs call on training managers and human resources executives, sellers of software call on information technology managers, sellers of manufacturing equipment call on plant managers, and so on. All are in search of the sole decision maker, a mythical character who, for all practical purposes, does not exist in the complex sale.

The problem with this fixation on job titles is twofold. First, every salesperson in your industry is calling on the same person inside the customer's organization, so that person has had significant practice at putting up barriers and restricting access. Even when contact is made, salespeople's ability to establish themselves as unique is severely impacted. Because of the frequency with which the "usual suspects" must deal with salespeople, they are usually immune to even the best moves. Second, the usual suspects are often not the best initial contact. It isn't unusual to find a major disconnect between the individuals who are experiencing the impact of the problem and those who are tasked to buy the solution. Typically, we find that it is middle managers who are busy avoiding buying decisions while unidentified individuals at the executive and operational levels of the organization are experiencing the consequences of the problem and the impact of the absence of the salesperson's solutions.

Successful sales professionals, on the other hand, tend to enter customer organizations through less obvious and more productive avenues of access. They identify the best entry points by determining who in the customer's organization is experiencing the impact of the absence of what they can provide. That, most likely, is an individual whose ability to accomplish personal and professional goals is being restricted by the problem or lack of solution. For instance, one

---

Key Thought
The Victim Is Much More Receptive and
Communicative Than the Perpetrator

The individuals in the business who are adversely affected by a business problem or inefficiency are much more receptive to discussing it, and the impact, than the individuals who may be the cause of the problem.

of our clients provides automated manufacturing systems that place components on printed circuit boards. Manufacturing or production engineers typically purchase these machines and the manufacturing lines they are in; therefore, every salesperson initiates contact there. As we worked with this client to develop an optimal entry strategy, it was determined that the early warning indicator is their prospective customer's losing bids or turning down bids because of lack of ability to place certain size components. The victim in this example, or the person most acutely aware if this is occurring, is the salesperson who is turning away the business. A call to a customer's salesperson was very simple. The equipment salesperson explained the nature of the call, "I'm trying to determine if your organization is experiencing this issue, and if so, would it make any sense to discuss it further with your management?" The diagnostic questions determined that this company was in fact turning away business, which quickly led to a calculation of the financial impact; a suggestion was made to talk with the regional manager. (Is this an isolated case, or is it happening to other salespeople in other territories?) It was determined that the salesforce had been forced to turn down $8 million of new business because current equipment could not handle a certain component that our client's equipment was capable of placing on circuit boards. With the cost of the problem in hand, the regional sales executive brought the salesperson to the vice president of sales, who took him to the vice president of operations, who in turn called in the manufacturing engineers and told them to make the sale happen.

In this example, a manufacturing engineer, who is more isolated from the company's customers, sees little value in the new capability of the salesperson's equipment, but the sales executive knows that customers would buy if they could build the boards with the special component. Likewise, a

> **Key Thought**
> **Who Gets the Call in the Middle of the Night?**
>
> Prime salespeople seek to enter the organization through the door of the person who is experiencing the symptoms of the problem in a way that would be most likely to drive a decision to change. When they identify the person "who gets the call in the middle of the night," they've found the person who cares most about the problems their offerings address.

processing plant manager who already has a set amount of downtime built into this year's budget may have little interest in spending unbudgeted funds for automated control equipment that promises to reduce the downtime next year. Executives at the corporate level, who would see the increased production capacity in future years drop straight to the organization's bottom line, would be operating from a completely different perspective. Again, the optimum entry point may likely be the nontraditional choice.

Answering the Customer's Questions

Once you have identified the person who represents the best point of entry to a potential customer, it is time to initiate the first formal contact. Many books have been written about this initial contact. They cover telephone skills and conversational gambits aimed at one thing—getting the appointment. Unfortunately, most miss the most important consideration in the initial customer contact.

Successful salespeople think beyond simply setting the appointment. Their goal in the initial conversation is to determine if this customer is the optimal place to invest their resources at this time. The more resources they involve in the initial appointment, the more scrutiny they give this conversation. They want to get invited into the right customer's organization by the right people for the right reasons. The real secret to "getting invited in" is in approaching your first conversation from the customer's perspective and by focusing the content of your call exclusively on the customer's situation. Prime salespeople don't initiate contact by talking at length about their companies, their offerings, or themselves. They introduce and describe themselves through the issues that they address, not through the solutions they offer, *diagnostic positioning.*

Any time a prospective customer picks up the telephone and speaks to a salesperson for the first time, the customer is seeking answers to a short sequence of questions. The key to being invited in is in offering customers the information they need to answer each question—no more and no less. If the customer is able to answer questions in a positive way, the result is continued interaction. If not, the conversation is over. The questions that customers ask themselves are simple, and the answers they infer are considered from only one point of view—their own:

- Should I talk with this person?
- Is this call relevant to my situation?
- Is this something we should discuss further?

To talk or not to talk? That is the question and the starting point of all conversations. It's a basic decision, and its answer is determined on basic information. You know what makes you decide not to talk—the mispronounced name, the rapid-fire delivery, or the canned spiel. Consider the things that make customers decide to stay on the line with a salesperson. Certainly, the sound of the salesperson's voice is one. Does this person have a professional tone—relaxed, not rushed? And, what about the introductory statements callers use? Does the caller say the customer's name? Has the caller been referred by someone the customer knows? Is the caller talking to the customer or reading from a page? Does the caller suggest that the conversation that is about to ensue may not be appropriate? (Suggesting to customers that the call may be inappropriate is an empowering statement. It immediately relaxes the customer and actually begins the conversation with agreement. It also suggests that the salesperson will not pressure them if they feel that there is no value in the conversation.)

All of this adds up to a single judgment in the customer's mind: Does this caller sound and act like a professional, like a colleague? When we sound professional, customers stay on the line. When we don't, they don't.

The next question customers consider is whether the call is relevant to their current situation. Customers want to know if we understand their world, and we need to prove that we do. Here, successful salespeople begin to demonstrate the knowledge they have obtained about the customer's industry and company. If you were in the customer's shoes, you would want to know if the caller typically works with (as opposed to sells to) people like you. What kinds of issues do the salesperson's solutions typically align with? Do these issues concern the customer? Once this information is communicated, the customer is ready to make the final decision in the initial contact.

The final question customers consider is whether the initial contact should be extended. They are trying to figure out if this salesperson can add to their understanding of the problem at hand. The customer often asks questions such as, "How can you help me?" Conventional salespeople are very happy to begin presenting solution ideas now, but Prime salespeople take a step back and begin to describe the diagnostic process through which they will guide the customer. At this point, they begin to establish the ground rules for further engagement.

Establishing a Diagnostic Agreement

The final task of the Discover phase is the establishment of a diagnostic agreement. Diagnostic agreements are informal, verbal agreements between the sales professional and the customer that lay out the ground rules for a constructive engagement. The agreement prepares for the beginning of the Diagnose phase of the Prime Process. A diagnostic agreement sets a professional tone for the continued conversations between the salesperson and the customer and sets the stage for open, unfettered communication. This is accomplished by setting limits on future conversations, thus assuring customers that they will not be forced into situations in which they are not comfortable.

The effective diagnostic agreement explicitly defines parameters for continued conversations, a proposed agenda, the participants, and feedback plans. It sets up the flow and specifies individuals who should be involved and topics to be covered. It also specifies mutual "homework"—what facts and figures we need to check for symptoms of the customer's problem, what information and resources the customer will bring to the meeting, and what information and resources the salesperson will bring. This is unique in the sales world where getting in the door is usually considered the ultimate goal of the first contact, but it is a standard feature in other professions such as law, medicine, and consulting. When we assign homework, we cause customers to begin to think about their situations, the specific symptoms of their problems, and the impact they have. We involve them ahead of the engagement, and we signal our intent to discuss their situation in more detail.

After the salesperson and the customer create a diagnostic agreement, the Discover phase is complete. The salesperson knows that he or she is spending time in the best place, and customers know that they are dealing with a professional who can be trusted and will treat them ethically and with respect.

Discovery is a term used by lawyers to describe the process of gathering information on which they will build their arguments. Because we've borrowed that term from the legal profession, it is only fair to let a lawyer have the last word about this phase of the Prime Process. Gerry Spence, who regularly appears on news programs as a legal analyst and is the "winningest trial lawyer in America," devotes a full chapter in his book, *How to Argue and Win Every Time*, to the importance of case preparation. He pegs his success to the fact that he spends more time than his opponents to prepare to enter the courtroom. Spence, who has never lost a criminal case, declares: "Prepare. Prepare. Prepare. And win."[2]

5

Diagnose the Complex Problem

The Optimal Source of Differentiation

The core competency of the complex sale is the Prime sales professional's ability to perform as an expert diagnostician. This diagnostic expertise enables us to help customers analyze and understand the causes and consequences of their problems, a critical prerequisite of a high-quality decision. Equally important, it allows us to shift the emphasis of our engagement with customers from our solutions to their situations, a shift that differentiates us from our competitors, creates significant learning for the customer, and builds the levels of trust and credibility through which our customers perceive us.

These outcomes stand in stark contrast to the conventional sales process, which depends on customers to understand and communicate their problems to salespeople. Popular and rarely questioned selling strategies such as consultative selling, needs-based selling, solution selling, and even value-added selling all depend to a large degree on the customer's ability to self-diagnose and self-prescribe, an expertise that we have already shown is in short supply. Largely, customers are not experienced in diagnosing complex problems, designing complex solutions, and implementing complex solutions.

The assumption that customers can and should be diagnosing themselves causes further damage when salespeople, thinking that their customers understand their problems and the need to resolve them, prematurely focus on solutions. Describing solutions without establishing a compelling need for them creates intellectual interest and curiosity among customers instead of the emotional discomfort needed to drive change. As a result, the conventional salesperson wastes time and effort on the intellectually curious customer, while the economically serious customer, who is actually experiencing the indications and/or consequences of the absence of the solution, stands by unrecognized and unattended.

When we salespeople are in the diagnostic mode, we are dealing directly with our customers' reality. That is, we are working with problems that they have experienced in the past, are currently experiencing, or to which they believe they will be exposed in the future. In fact, our customers may not be aware that they have these problems and might be missing a significant opportunity. As we discussed in Chapter 3, when customers realize that they are dealing with real problems and real costs (as opposed to future benefits), the urgency that drives the decision to change is created. They find themselves on the critical, actionable end of the change progression. Diagnosis, as it methodically uncovers real problems and expands the customer's awareness, causes the customer to move along the change progression.

Our ability to diagnose customer problems sets us apart from the competition. Most salespeople devote themselves to establishing *expected* credibility. They lean on the presentation of their company's brands, history, and reputation. The irony of this approach is that it makes them sound like everyone else (and reinforces the trend toward commoditization). This conclusion is validated repeatedly in our seminars when we ask participants how much their "credibility story" differs from their top competitors' stories. Only a few are willing to stand and declare that there are significant differences. The ability and willingness to diagnose will provide a significant difference between our competitors and us. It gives us the opportunity to establish *exceptional* credibility in our customers' eyes.

The quest for exceptional credibility in the Diagnose phase of the Prime Process has two primary goals. The first is to uncover the reality of the customer's problem. The professional salesperson cannot and will not recommend a solution without first confirming that the customer is actually experiencing the problems it is meant to solve or is poised to capitalize on the opportunity the solution represents.

The second, and more important goal of the Diagnose phase, is to make sure that the customer fully and accurately perceives all the ramifications of the problem, the absence of the solution. The decision to buy is the customer's decision, and the only way to ensure the quality of that decision is to ensure that the customer fully understands the problem and the consequences of staying the same. This is analogous to the job of the psychiatrist. An experienced psychiatrist may be able to diagnose a patient's mental illness after a single visit. After all, the doctor has treated many other patients who suffer from the same disease. Yet, it may take several sessions before the patient believes he or she has a problem and believes that the doctor also understands that problem. Psychiatrists know that until patients come to those realizations, they will have no credibility in patients' eyes, and the path to a cure will remain blocked.

When salespeople fail to reach either goal of the Diagnose phase, their ability to win complex sales is severely compromised. The outcome of the sale becomes as random and unpredictable as the results of the conventional selling process. When we don't diagnose a complex problem, we have no basis for designing and delivering a high-quality solution. If we diagnose complex problems, but don't help our customers to fully comprehend them, they will not see the need for change and will not buy. Successful sales professionals strive to recognize and achieve both goals of a comprehensive diagnosis for all of these reasons.

The raw information that we need to make an accurate diagnosis comes primarily from the customer; thus, the quality of the sales professional's questions becomes the primary skill of the information-gathering process. The value

---

Key Thought
You Gain More Credibility from the
Questions You Ask Than the Stories You Tell

Conventional salespeople tell stories about their solutions. Prospective customers expect to hear these stories and rarely take them seriously. What is taken seriously is the concern and expertise we display in the questions we ask customers. The right questions form the basis for customer opinions concerning how well salespeople understand customers' problems, whether they can help customers expand their own knowledge of the problems, and how likely they are to be the best source for the solution.

---

of asking questions is also predicated on another important skill, *listening*. Noted doctor and author Oliver Sacks states: "There is one cardinal rule: One must always listen to the patient."[1] Questions are more than tools to elicit information, however. When questions are being asked and answered, the customer is forming opinions that will be critical to the outcome of the decision.

Prime salespeople are guiding their customers to four elemental decisions in the Diagnose phase; they are deciding:

1. That a problem does indeed exist.
2. That they want to participate in a thorough analysis of the problem.
3. That the problem has a quantifiable cost in their organization.

4. Whether that cost dictates they must proceed in the search for a solution.

When we help our customers successfully complete these decisions, it is highly likely that we have earned exceptional credibility in their eyes and have stepped into the customer's world as a full-fledged business partner "and a source of business advantage." We next take a closer look at how Prime sales professionals help customers make these decisions.

Establishing the Critical Perspective

In the complex sale, we work with multiple individuals in the customer's organization to develop a comprehensive view of the situation. Each of these individuals has some of the information we need to diagnose the problem, and each has a unique perspective. It is a lot like the often-told story of the blind men and the elephant. Each man approached the elephant at a different point and, as a result, each described the animal in a radically different way.

To communicate most effectively with each of the individuals who has information about a complex problem, to obtain the best information they have to offer, and to evaluate the validity of that information, we first must consider the critical perspective of that person. We need to understand the mind-set and position from which they are seeing the symptoms of the problem.

We ask three questions designed to help us understand a person's critical perspective:

1. *What is this person's education and career background?* In Chapter 4, we talked about how the background of an

organization's leaders can affect the way the entire organization thinks. So, too, the background of an individual colors his or her personal perspective of the world. A person with an education in accounting approaches and perceives a problem differently than a person educated in marketing. Further, uncovering the professional and educational disciplines that influence a person's thinking can be particularly helpful when you are working with senior management, where a person's background is often not directly related to his or her current job.

2. *What are this person's job responsibilities?* An individual's critical perspective is going to be intimately linked with his or her current goals and duties. Certainly, personal concerns about job security and performance are among the most powerful forces at work on the change spectrum. Salespeople should always remember that it is easier for them to find a new customer than it is for their customers to find new jobs.

3. *What are the work issues and problems that concern this person?* We often find salespeople trying to engage customers in issues and problems that exist outside an individual's area of responsibility or that may not exist at all in the customer's critical perspective. For instance, a director of quality who is charged with maintaining unit defects at a consistent Six Sigma level perceives an innovative new solution for speeding the manufacturing process from a different perspective than does a plant manager who is charged with obtaining higher output. The former is perfectly happy with the status quo (if it has reached Six Sigma) and highly resistant to any change that could threaten it, while the latter sees the status quo as a performance problem that must be addressed.

Salespeople will begin to understand customers' worry lists—their individual job concerns and issues—by asking themselves about the typical concerns of individuals with this particular job title. The director of quality is concerned with issues such as product defects, process reliability, and customer satisfaction. As soon as we get face-to-face with this person, we must confirm the existence of those concerns and narrow our focus on specific areas of dissatisfaction.

The conventional approach to selling depends on laundry lists of questions that focus on needs and solutions. The disadvantage of this process is that the salesperson may not connect with concerns until a dozen or more questions have been asked, long after the customer's patience has worn thin. In Prime Process diagnosis, we use an A-to-Z question, which is designed to instantly bring to the surface the customer's most serious concern.

For example, assume that you are a sales executive exploring the sales performance programs provided by The Prime Resource Group. As you read the question, think about the answer you would give. We would ask: "As you consider your sales process . . . beginning with generating a new lead . . . moving on through all the interactions with a customer . . . and finally, ending up with a profitable new customer . . . if you had to choose one part of the entire sales process that concerns you the most . . . as well as things are going for you . . . what concern would you put at the top of your list?"

Before we discuss your answer, look at the question again. This is a long question, and the way it is asked, with plenty of pauses with a long thoughtful look or two at the ceiling, makes it even longer. There is good reason for that. We are pacing the customer's thinking process, giving him time to create a thoughtful response. It is designed to frame the customer's thinking within a certain process in his job responsibility. Another important element of the A-to-Z question is that it sounds spontaneous, not like the typical canned question. It is designed to elicit thoughtful consideration and a meaningful response from the customer.

There is one more element to address—the phrase "as well as things are going for you." This defuses any defensiveness the customer is feeling. Without a phrase like this, a likely response could be: "Things are going quite well, thank you." By acknowledging and complimenting customers' past successes, you are suggesting that with their success, they are perhaps interested in getting even better. The phrase eliminates the customer's need to defend or proclaim past success.

Returning to the previous question, did you think about the question; did it trigger a review of your sales process? Did you believe the question was sincere and try to address it seriously? Most people do. In fact, when we ask A-to-Z questions, we stop and listen. Silence is good. The longer the silence lasts, the better the answer is. The A-to-Z question is a most effective means of getting to the heart of the issue.

Peeling the Onion

In a perfect world, salespeople and customers communicate openly, honestly, and with complete clarity about the problems the customer is experiencing. But we don't work in a perfect world. In the real world of complex sales, customers are often unaware of the full extent of their problems; even when they do understand them, they are just as often reluctant to share that information. Salespeople don't usually ask what they really want to know first, and customers don't usually say what they really mean first. This lack of openness, which we all exhibit to one degree or another, is a natural and common protective behavior that has evolved from childhood.

When we communicate through the critical perspective of our customers, we begin to overcome the barriers to communication. Empathy, however, is not enough. Our customers need to be assured that it is safe to share information with us and that we will not use the information they provide to manipulate them. We communicate that assurance by our willingness to walk away from an engagement whenever the facts dictate that there is no fit between the customer's situation and our offerings. This is no sacrifice on the salesperson's part. When we spend time with a customer who has no problem, we simply waste our most valuable resource—our time.

The second way we assure our customers that we can be trusted is to approach a diagnosis at the customer's pace. Leading a witness is forbidden in a courtroom and should also be forbidden in the complex sale. Customers must discover, understand the impact of, and take ownership of problems before deciding to seek a solution. Yet, customers rarely reach conclusions about their problems at the same time that salespeople do. When salespeople move too quickly and too far ahead of their customers, they create a gap that customers often see as applying pressure or manipulation. The result is mistrust and a confrontational atmosphere.

Crossing customers' emotional barriers to get to the heart of the issues that concern them is like peeling an onion. When we "peel the onion," we accomplish two goals. First, we pass through the layers of protection that customers use to shield themselves from the potentially negative impact of open communication. We move from cliché (which is the surface level of emotion) through

---

Key Thought
The Three Most Important Words in
Communication: Nurture, Nurture, and Nurture

People reveal their true feelings and problems only
when they believe that their input will be respected
and no negative consequences will result from the information they share. Prime salespeople are careful to
communicate by word and deed that they mean customers no harm. This nurturing attitude enables open
communication and mutual understanding and maximizes the probability of a quality decision.

---

levels of fact and opinion to the most powerful driver of
change—true feelings.

We peel the onion using a series of deliberately struc-
tured questions, which we call a *diagnostic map*. Too often,
salespeople ask questions simply to prolong conversations
until they can create openings to present their solutions.
The result is surface communication and superficial engagement. The diagnostic map, on the other hand, is designed to explore issues in an accurate and efficient way
while creating the trust needed to elicit forthright answers
from our customers.

One way we move through a diagnostic map is with
the *assumptive* question. Assumptive questions are phrased
in a way that assumes the customer is capable and knowl-
edgeable. It is a good way to communicate respect and en-
gender trust. This phrasing is very important.

When we worked with a company selling disaster recovery software, we found that its salespeople were using a slide
presentation designed to educate their clients about the risks
they were incurring without their software. One slide boldly

stated: "Eighty percent of companies under 50 MM in sales do not have disaster recovery systems." The salesperson would then ask, "Do you?" If you were the customer confronted with such a question, how would you react?

In contrast, we designed an assumptive question to address the same situation: "When you put together your disaster recovery plan, which of the potential bottlenecks gave you the most concern?" This implies that the customer knows his or her business, and because it assumes the best, the customer is complimented by that assumption and it makes the customer feel safe enough to admit that there is no plan in place. It has the added benefit of introducing the idea that the customer might be exposed to a serious, and thus far, unaddressed risk. The sequence of thoughts the customer goes through is (1) feeling complimented, (2) realizing they haven't considered the issue, and (3) recognizing the sales professional has added considerable value by introducing a topic that should not be overlooked, thus creating trust of the sales professional, concern for the issue, and credibility of the sales professional in preventing a flawed decision.

The second goal of peeling the onion is to establish the existence and extent of the problem itself. Again, questions play the starring role in this work. A second type of question, the *indicator* question, is used to identify the symptoms of the kinds of problems our offerings are designed to solve. An indicator is a physical signal. It is a recognizable event, occurrence, or situation that can be seen, heard, or perceived by the customer. It doesn't require an expert opinion, and we are not asking the customer to self-diagnose. Instead, we are simply asking for an observation.

The difference between opinion and observation is important; the easiest way to make it clear is to look to the medical profession. If a heart surgeon made a diagnosis as a conventional salesperson does, it might sound like this:

SURGEON: "So, how are you feeling today?"

PATIENT: "Great. I feel good."

SURGEON: "Have you been thinking about doing anything with your heart?"

PATIENT: "Well, quite a few of my friends have been having heart surgery. So I thought maybe I should consider it, too!"

SURGEON: "Are you leaning toward angioplasty or bypass?"

It's a silly exchange, but notice that it is based on self-diagnosis. The doctor is asking the patient for an expert opinion, and that is exactly what the conventional salesperson does. In reality, doctors don't put much value in patients' opinions, but they do value patients' observations. They ask indicator questions, such as "Have you noticed any shortness of breath lately?" and "Have you experienced any dizziness or numbness?" These questions ask the patient for an observation and lead to additional questions and a more in-depth diagnosis.

At this point, the salespeople who attend our seminars often ask what to do if no problem indicators are present in a customer's organization. The answer is simple: The engagement is over, or at least the diagnosis is postponed until such indicators appear. If there are no indicators, there is no problem. No problem means no pain; thus, the probability that the customer will make a decision to change is very low. It is time for the salesperson to move this customer into his or her opportunity management system and engage new customers who are experiencing the indicators of the problems he or she solves.

Another tool for tapping into the desire to be understood is a question called the *conversation expander*. Like indicator questions, these questions give our customers the

---

Key Thought
No Pain—No Change, No Change—No Sale

When indicators are present, however, we continue the questioning process to expand our own—and the customer's—understanding of the problem. We continue peeling the onion and exposing the full dimensions of the problem by creating sequences of linked questions. We link questions by building each new question on the customer's answer to the previous question. When we do this, we are encouraging further explanation and additional detail. Communications experts tell us that humans have a natural desire to be understood. With each new question, we tap into that desire in our customers and together reach a deeper understanding and a greater level of clarity about the problem.

---

opportunity to expand on explanations and clarify their thoughts. We can ask them at any stage of the Prime Process. Examples for use during problem analysis are shown in Figure 5.1.

We ask diagnostic questions to establish a chain of causality. Indicators represent the symptoms of a problem, but symptoms represent only clues to actual causes of a problem. As any doctor will tell you, eliminating the symptoms of a problem does not solve the problem. For instance, a patient may use an antacid to ease the pain caused by an ulcer, but the antacid does not cure the ulcer nor does it address the causes of the ulcer. In fact, eliminating symptoms often masks the problem and even exacerbates them, enabling the problem to continue undetected.

Indicator Expansion

Could you expand a bit on . . . ?

Tell me more about . . .

You mentioned a concern about . . . Could you walk me through that?

Could you help me understand . . . ?

Example of Situation

What would be an example of . . . ?

Could you give me an example of . . . ?

What would an example of . . . look like in your business/industry?

I'm not clear how . . . works. Can you give an example?

Duration

When did you first start to experience . . . ?

When did you first notice . . . ?

Has . . . been happening for long?

How often does . . . happen?

FIGURE 5.1   **Conversational Expanders**

We identify the causes of problems by asking questions about their indicators. When we determine the causes of a problem, we have also reached causes of the customer's dissatisfaction. That dissatisfaction is the vehicle that drives the decision to change, but simply establishing the existence of a problem is not a complete diagnosis.

Calculating the Cost of the Problem

Salespeople can do a thorough job of establishing and communicating the symptoms and causes of customers' problems, present viable solutions to those problems, and still walk away from the engagement empty-handed. This outcome most often occurs when salespeople ignore a crucial piece of the diagnostic process—connecting a dollar value to the consequences of the problem.

Problems run rampant in organizations. Some are not significant enough in consequences or risk to address; others must be addressed because their consequences or risks are too high. The fact that a problem exists is not enough to ensure change. When the customer does not know the actual cost of a problem, the success of winning the complex sale is severely compromised.

Typically, customers do not quantify the costs of complex problems on their own. The main reason for this, as we saw in Chapter 2, is that most customers simply don't have

---

Key Thought
Pain Is the Vehicle That Drives the Decision
—The Cost of the Pain Is the Accelerator!

When we define the cost of the problem, we put a price tag on the dissatisfaction the customer is experiencing. That tag enables customers to prioritize the problem and then make a rational, informed choice between continuing to incur its cost and investing in a solution. In fact, as we see in the next chapter, establishing an accurate cost of the problem is the only path to defining the true value of a solution. Cost is also the surest way to shorten the customer's decision cycle. Think of the customer's pain as the decision driver and the cost of the pain as its accelerator. The higher the cost of the problem, the faster the decision to solve it.

the expertise required to fix those costs. Even when they do attempt to quantify their problems, they usually focus on the surface costs and tend to overlook the total cost.

Salespeople also tend to shy away from fixing costs. Many complain that it is too hard to determine, but we find that the real reason is that they are afraid that the cost of the problem will be too low to be addressed and the engagement will be over. They are reluctant to do anything that might interfere with "going for the yes." This is always a possible outcome, and it is a legitimate one. If the cost of a customer's problem does not justify the solutions being offered, the professional will acknowledge that reality and (in the spirit of "always be leaving") move on to a better qualified customer. If this happens too often, the salesperson and his or her organization have a larger problem—solutions are too expensive in terms of the value they offer customers.

Another common objection to cost calculation that we hear from salespeople is that their offerings are not meant to solve problems. They say that they provide new opportunities; therefore, they can't fix the costs. This is not a valid objection. There are no free moves in business. There are

---

Key Thought
If You Don't Have a Cost of the Problem, You Don't Have a Problem
If There Is No Problem, There Is No Value

All businesses measure their performance in dollars and cents. Therefore, any problem they are experiencing or opportunity they are missing can be expressed in financial terms. Until you quantify that impact, you are dealing with a highly speculative issue.

always costs present in every decision. Even when a solution offers a new capability, there is still a cost if the customer chooses not to adopt it.

When salespeople explore the total cost of a problem, they need to use a combination of three types of figures:

1. *Direct numbers:* Established or known figures.

2. *Indirect numbers:* Inferred or estimated figures.

3. *Lost opportunities:* Figures representing the options that customers cannot pursue because of the resources consumed by the problem.

When we talk about the total cost of the problem, we are not saying that you must establish a precise figure. Rather, the cost must be generally accurate. Calculating costs is a process similar to the navigational method known as triangulation. By sighting off of three points—the direct numbers, indirect numbers, and lost opportunities—we can arrive at a cost that is accurate and, most importantly, believed by the customer (see Figure 5.2).

FIGURE 5.2   **Cost of the Problem**

This is accomplished in two steps. First, we salespeople need to provide a formula that is conceptually sound. Second, we must ensure that the numbers plugged into that formula are derived from the customer's reality, not the salesperson's. We know we have successfully completed these steps when our customers are willing to defend the validity of the cost among their own colleagues.

The following example shows how a cost conversation works. A salesperson in the shoplifting detection equipment industry calls on independent pharmacies. He engages the owner of a drugstore with revenues of $1.5 million, who is experiencing the industry average shrinkage of 3 percent. This tells the salesperson that the store is losing $45,000 annually to some combination of customer theft, employee theft, and sloppy inventory management. The store manager, who does not believe that the store is experiencing any significant customer theft because the store is in a "better part of town," is not interested in the salesperson's offering.

The salesperson agrees with the customer's point (atmosphere of cooperation) and then asks an Indicator question, "Do you ever notice empty packages on the floor?" The store manager replies, "You have a point there, but it's not enough to be worried about." "Probably not," the salesperson replies and then asks the next question to establish an indirect number. "Out of every 100 people in this community, how many do you think would shoplift?" The curious manager replies, "One percent, 1 out of 100."

The salesperson now asks for a series of direct and indirect numbers, such as the number of buying customers in the store each day and the ratio of buying customers to browsers. They yield a figure of 533 people in the store each day. The salesperson asks, "What do you think the average cost of a shoplifting incident would be?" The manager replies, "$15."

From this information, the salesperson calculates that there are five shoplifters in the store each day, and the average daily loss is $75. Further, the store is open 365 days each year, making the annual loss $27,000—a believable figure in light of the store's $45,000 annual shrinkage.

The detection equipment costs $15,000 to install and $2,000 per year to operate. Subtracted from the cost of the store's problem, this yields a positive return of $10,000 the first year and $25,000 in subsequent years. Over three years, the lost opportunity is $20,000 per year.[2]

As you can see, we develop the data used to determine costs the same way we explore problems—through the process of diagnostic questioning. The answers to our questions tell us whether our customers have the resources and willingness to solve their problems. More importantly, the process of answering questions allows our customers to reach their own conclusions in their own time. Further, the fact that the customer provides the data enhances the credibility of the cost conclusions that result. This creates a high level of buy-in. It is also more compelling and accurate than the generic cost/return formulas and average industry costs that we so often find in conventional sales presentations.

Remember, it is the responsibility of the sales professional to develop the "cost of the problem" formula. It is a critical component of the quality decision process that they bring to their customer. The customer does not have the expertise or the inclination to put such a formula together. It will provide you with a key differentiator.

The final element of the Diagnose phase is to determine the problem's priority in the customer's mind. This is one crucial test of the significance of a problem's consequences that salespeople often overlook. The fact that a problem's costs are substantial in the salesperson's eyes does not guarantee that the customer feels the same way or will attempt to resolve it.

he cost may be an accepted part of doing busi-
ail chain includes a line item for inventory
n its annual budget; a manufacturing plant
me level of defects acceptable. Unless the cost
exceeds acceptable levels, salespeople may well find that
the customer will not feel the need to make a decision
to change.

Second, even when costs do exceed acceptable levels,
they must still be compelling in light of the other critical
issues vying for the resources of the organization. If, for example, a customer is confronting a shrinking market for the
goods or services the salesperson's offerings address and, as
a result, has decided to leave that business, there is little
reason to invest additional resources no matter how compelling the cost savings.

This is why it is so important to ask the customer to
prioritize the problem and its costs before moving out of
the Diagnose phase of the Prime Process. Again, this information is developed by asking questions, such as conversation expanders (see Figure 5.3).

Cost Quantification

Have you had a chance to put a number on . . . ?

What does your experience tell you . . . is costing?

Can you give a ball park number as to what . . . costs?

Cost Prioritization

How does . . . compare to other issues you are dealing with?

Does it make sense to go after a solution to . . . at this time?

When you consider all the other issues on your desk, where does . . .
fall?

FIGURE 5.3 Conversation Expanders: Cost of the Problem

The Buying Decision

The Diagnose phase is now complete. In summary:

- As salespeople, we have helped customers to realize that they have a problem that is seriously affecting their personal and/or business objectives.
- With our assistance, the customer has thoroughly explored the dimensions of the problem and assigned a total cost to it.
- The customer has determined whether that cost justifies immediate action relative to other issues and opportunities they face.
- If we are still in the room at this point in the engagement, it is for one reason only: The customer has made the decision to buy.
- We have not made a sales presentation. In fact, we haven't devoted any significant time to describing our solutions at all.
- We haven't exerted any pressure on the customer whatsoever. Nevertheless, the customer has decided there is a problem that is costing more than he or she is willing to absorb and that we, the salespeople, understand the situation.

It is very important to recognize:

1. You don't need to have a solution to have a problem and
2. You don't need to have a solution to diagnose a problem.

Introducing solutions too early will frequently diffuse the decision process and distract from a clear diagnosis.

One of the keys to managing the decision process is staying true to the decision at hand.

3. We have the inside track on this sale.

How did this happen? It resulted from a simple, logical change progression that has taken place in the customer's mind:

- There is a problem.
- It costs a fixed amount of money to leave it unattended.
- That amount of money is significant enough to act on.
- That decision to act is the decision to solve the problem or, more directly, the decision to buy a solution.

At the same time customers are reaching the critical stage in the change progression, salespeople have been establishing their own value in the customer's eyes. They have earned the customer's professional respect because of their ability to conduct a high-quality diagnosis. The customer's trust is gained because of the salesperson's willingness to end the engagement at any time the diagnosis revealed that a problem did not exist or was not worth acting on. The salesperson has created exceptional credibility by demonstrating an in-depth understanding of the customer's business. Now that the customer has made the decision to change, who do you think the customer believes is best qualified to help design a high-quality solution to the problem?

Granted the customer may not openly announce their decision, but they will present a more open and trusting demeanor. Signs such as answering questions very openly

> ### Key Thought
> ### The Decision to Change, to Buy, and from
> ### Whom Is Made During the Diagnosis
>
> The conventional salesperson believes the decision to buy is made much later, after a presentation and proposal. One of the most significant paradigm shifts of the Prime Process is that as you conduct a thorough diagnosis, and by the time your customer has made the four elemental decisions of the Diagnose phase (see page 104), it is highly likely that the customer has already made their decision to change and to change what they will buy. Since you have established exceptional credibility, it is highly likely they have decided to buy from you and your company.

and providing access to people and information will verify and back up the fact that the decision has been made.

If you grab hold of this idea, and it is well-supported by our research, it will provide a profound change to your business. Your days of pre-mature presentations will be over, and your proposal conversion ratio will increase dramatically.

6

Designing the Complex Solution

Prevent Unpaid Consulting

In the *Design* phase of the Prime Process, we focus our efforts on the solutions to our customers' problems. Prime professionals guide the design process by managing expectations of the cast of characters. In this phase, they help their customers establish expectations about solution outcomes, determine the methods and alternatives for obtaining those outcomes, specify investment levels and implementation timing, define the criteria that will govern buying decisions, and build consensus and confirmation among the cast of characters within the customer's organization for the findings and decisions that have resulted from the diagnosis and design efforts. In short, we create and align the solution.

If you paid close attention to the preceding paragraph, you may have noticed that it says nothing about the products and services that salespeople are bringing to market. Instead, it focuses on defining the parameters of a high-quality solution. In the Design phase, we specify and confirm the customer's preferred outcomes and decision-making criteria, but we *do not* present solutions. This is a continuation of the spirit of partnership and collaboration that we have been building throughout the engagement.

Our methodology stands in stark contrast to conventional selling methodologies. In conventional selling, the only acceptable result of an engagement is the customer's buying the salesperson's offering. This statement dictates a fixed solution. When salespeople enter the engagement, they have this fixed end in mind: Regardless of the customer's situation and requirements, the conventional salesperson is focused on only one solution—his or her own. Given this pre-established outcome, is it any wonder that so many customers perceive sales engagements as zero-sum games and think of salespeople as being willing to use any means to achieve their ends?

Prime professionals approach the solution phase of the complex sale as an exploratory process. The aim is to equip the customer to make the best, most effective choice among the solutions competing in the marketplace. This is not to say that Prime professionals approach an engagement without a preferred solution in mind. Like other salespeople, they are in business to sell their products and services. They understand, however, that their offerings are not always the best solution for the customer, and they recommend only offerings that are in the best interests of the customer. As always, they apply the "do no harm" principle of the doctor and integrity test of the best friend. If Prime professionals' offerings do not fill the bill, they are the first to recognize and acknowledge that fact and even recommend a more appropriate source for the required solution. In this way, Prime professionals protect and retain their "valued advisor" status in the customer's mind and remain welcome to revisit the customer at a future date. At the same time, the salesperson has freed himself or herself and resources to move on to a more qualified customer.

While conventional salespeople often act as if competing solutions do not exist, Prime professionals discuss solution alternatives head-on. They know that in the competitive environment of the complex sale, customers will examine alternative solutions, and they also realize that actively participating in that examination is better than ignoring it. Given the fact that so many salespeople are afraid to act as if competing solutions exist, the open, customer-first attitude of the Prime professional often becomes a positive differentiating factor in and of itself.

When salespeople do join a customer's search for the best answer to problems, they take a seat on the same side of the table and act as partners instead of adversaries. Further,

Prime professionals use this opportunity to strengthen their position by ensuring that their customers can recognize the inherent advantages and disadvantages among the solution alternatives.

In a larger sense, the goal of the design phase is to minimize the risk of change for the customer. In the diagnosis phase, we maximized the customer's awareness of risk. That is, we helped them to fully comprehend the risk involved in not addressing their problems and in not changing. When that effort was successful, the customer "owned" his problem. In the design phase, which the customer enters prepared to make a change, we begin working to minimize the exposure to risk inherent in the act of changing. When this effort is successful, the customer will be happy to "own" the solution to the problem.

Customers are exposed to three kinds of solution risks, which salespeople need to consider when designing solution parameters: process risk, performance risk, and personal risk. Process risks are exposures that stem from the implementation and ongoing operation of a solution. Performance risks are exposures that stem from the outcomes

---

Key Thought
There Are No Free Moves

When it comes to deciding complex sales, no matter what solution the customer chooses, including your own, that solution will contain positive and negative aspects. When we willingly and openly explore alternative solutions and their ramifications from the customer's perspective, we exhibit integrity and strengthen the bonds of trust between our customers and ourselves.

produced by a solution. Personal risks are exposures that the members of the cast of characters incur when they lend their personal support to a solution. As we create and define the parameters of a high-quality solution, we need to anticipate how each of these three risks might impact the customer and be sure to communicate those exposures to the customer during the decision-making process.

To illustrate these risks, we consider financial accounting software. A process risk is the possibility that a customer buys and installs a new accounting software package, which crashes the organization's computer network. A performance risk is the possibility that the new software does not work and miscalculates the organization's financial results. A personal risk is the possibility that the problems caused by the new software cause the person who recommended the purchase to be fired or shuffled off to a much less wanted position in the organization.

Consider the risks a customer faces when buying your offerings. What are the process, performance, and personal risks? How do you address them during the sales engagement?

Managing the Customer's Expectations

The first point of focus in the Design phase is on our customers' desired outcomes. This is primarily a visioning process. We want to create a discussion that is centered on the future, at a point when the customer's problem has been solved. This portrait of the future helps us define the customer's expectations about the solution. We can sum up expectations in the answers to three questions for our customers:

1. What do you expect this desired state to look like?

2. How much do you expect to invest to attain the desired state?

3. When do you expect to have the desired state in place?

What Does the Desired State Look Like?

The easiest way to begin to define the parameters of a solution is to ask customers how they expect their situation to look after the problem is solved. This portrait of an imagined future produces a list of outcomes that customers expect from the solution. It gives us the basic information that we need to begin to define the standards by which those outcomes will be measured.

As always, questions are the most effective tool at our command. We add depth to the customer's vision for solution outcomes through our questions. For instance, when a customer says that *reliability* is a critical outcome, it is our cue to ask questions that generate more detail about that outcome. We need to establish a specific definition of *reliability* and an exact figure for its measurement. In the process of establishing those answers, we are creating a clear definition of the customer's expectations and a valuable guide to the best solution to the customer's problem.

In addition to preventing miscommunication, Prime professionals must also ensure that the customer's requirements of a solution are realistic and attainable. Just because we ask customers to define their expectations does not necessarily mean that we should or can accept whatever answers they offer. The outcomes they envision must be possible, and it is our job to ensure that fact by managing the formulation process.

Mismatches between customer expectations and reality are a common occurrence in sales, and too often

---

Key Thought
No Mind-Reading: Clarify All "Fat" and "Loaded" Words

Reliability is an example of what we call a *fat* or *loaded word*. So are words such as *quality, value, soon,* and *support.* Customers often use fat or loaded words to describe their expectations about solutions (as well as their problems), but the words themselves are vague and can easily cause misunderstandings. If our definition of *quality*, for instance, is a 5 percent defect rate and our customer's definition is a 2 percent rate, we are setting ourselves up for failure.

---

salespeople abdicate responsibility for resolving them. Instead of bringing the customer back to earth as soon as unreasonable expectations surface, salespeople, who are often reluctant to say anything that might disappoint the customer, pass that unpleasant task downstream to the service and support functions. As a result, the customer's expectations become fixed, and when reality finally strikes, the level of dissatisfaction is higher. There is little point in providing a solution to a customer if we have fostered exaggerated expectations about performance of the product or service (or delivery date or final cost, for that matter). The only results we can expect from such a sale are complaints, conflict, and, in many cases, permanent loss of the customer.

Defining realistic expectations, on the other hand, sets the stage for customer satisfaction and repeat business. By defining expectations in quantitative as well as qualitative terms, we protect our customers and ourselves from disappointments and conflicts that result from poorly defined and unrealistic expectations.

How Much Do You Expect to Invest to Make It Happen?

The next set of expectations we need to define is the set that centers around the size of the investment our customers are willing to make to solve their problems.

In the Diagnose phase, we assigned a cost to the customer's problem. In the Design phase, we use that cost to calculate the value of the solution. This does *not* mean that it is time to talk about the price of our offerings or to begin negotiating price with the customer. Instead, we are going to quantify the financial impact of the desired outcome, that is, what the customer can expect in terms of increased revenues and/or decreased expenses. We want to determine what it is worth to the customer to solve the problem. The value of a solution and appropriate investment to obtain it can be expressed with two simple equations:

$$\underset{\text{(ROS)}}{\text{Return on solution}} - \underset{\text{(COP)}}{\text{Cost of problem}} = \text{Value}$$

$$\text{Value} \times \underset{\text{on investment (ROI)}}{\text{Customers expected return}} = \text{Investment}$$

When we help our customers calculate the worth of a solution, we set the financial parameters for a high-quality decision. Those parameters, which consider cost of the problem and return on investment the customer must earn on corporate resources, tell us how much is worth spending to resolve the problem.

Once those value parameters are set, it becomes very easy for the customer to evaluate the cost of solution alternatives. The actual cost of the solutions being offered becomes less important than how each solution's costs compares to the value the customer stands to gain. The ability to determine this information is a significant improvement over the typical way that customers approach price—a side-by-side comparison of solutions that tells the customer nothing about how much it is actually worth spending to solve the problem.

Defining investment expectations also serves the salesperson. First, because we already know the cost of our own offerings, it allows us to establish whether our solutions are financially feasible for the customer. If they are, the engagement continues. If not, the customer is returned to the salesperson's opportunity management system, and it is time to move on to a more qualified customer. Second, setting investment expectations largely eliminates price negotiations and objections about the price of our offerings. We know ahead of time that the investment required to purchase our solutions is a match with the customer's expectations.

Three common pitfalls that salespeople need to recognize and avoid in defining solution expectations are discussed in the following sections.

Key Thought
Budgets Are Not Cast in Stone

Conventional selling puts great weight on the customer's budget. Budgets are part of the corporate planning process. They represent management's desire to forecast and assign resources for anticipated needs. Conventional sales methods ignore the reality that the corporate budget is largely irrelevant in the complex sale.

Complex sales are investments. Corporate resources flow to the best investment, that is, the investment with the best return. In complex sales, budgets are altered and created; they rarely impede an attractive investment.

Key Thought *continued*

If we qualify based on an already-existing customer budget, it is highly likely that we are entering the complex sale too late. It may be possible to increase the customer's awareness that the problem is large enough to change the investment criteria. Our goal is to be working with customers when they create the investment criteria on which the budget is eventually based.

Premature Presentation

First, when customers begin talking about expectations, there is always a temptation, often an irresistible one, for the salesperson to slip into presentation. Customers say they expect high reliability as a solution outcome, and suddenly the salesperson is off and running with a speech about the consistent and reliable performance of the offering. We need to be aware of this and avoid the urge to present in the Design phase.

Unpaid Consulting

The second trap that often undermines salespeople during the Design phase is the trap of unpaid consulting. Unpaid consulting starts when we cross the line between defining parameters of a solution and creation of the design of the solution itself. When we start designing solutions, we start acting as consultants. In past decades, this was not a monumental issue. Generally, there was limited competition in complex sales. If you figured out the problem and designed a unique and competent solution for a customer, the sale was almost guaranteed and the salesperson was rewarded for his or her consulting effort. Ironically, many sales organizations continue that strategy and, for some reason, choose to ignore the fact that the environmental conditions that made that strategy successful in the past, for the most part, no longer exist. Today, there is an ever-increasing proliferation of competitors in the complex sale, and once a solution is designed, the customer can easily shop it to the competition. When that happens, we become unpaid consultants and our own worst enemies. We've enabled our competitor, who did not have the design investment, to provide the solution at a lower price. We can avoid that trap by staying focused on the customer's expectations for solution outcomes and not straying into the design of solutions. If you are providing true consulting that is transportable to competitors for fulfillment, you must extend your business model to include fees for professional services, and you must decide at what stage of the decision process the line between required diagnosis and design and paid consulting exists.

Creeping Elegance

The final trap is sprung when customers become so enthusiastic about the potential value of solutions to their problems that they expand the scope of the outcomes. When customers drop into this "as long as we're going to do this, we might as well also do that" mode of thinking, they tend to lose their sense of fiscal responsibility and conventional salespeople start to count the extra commissions.

The problem with this response lies in the very nature of the complex sale. There is no single decision maker in this sale, so when a salesperson allows one member of the cast of characters to unnecessarily expand the scope of a solution, you can be sure that the entire project will be shot down by the other members of the cast.

Prime professionals ensure that their sales do not expand beyond reasonable financial parameters. The rule they follow is: Never allow an expectation that is not backed up by a specific problem *and* a cost that supports the additional investment.

Timing: When Do You Expect to Have the Desired State in Place?

The final set of customer expectations is based on the timing of the expected outcomes. These are relatively simple to establish and don't require much explanation, but they are important. After all, in today's fast-changing world, a solution that arrives late can cause as much damage as one that does not arrive at all.

The customer's expectations as to solution timing tell us when the solution must be in place and the timetable on which it must be producing results. Further, timing expectations have the added benefit of signaling the customer's intentions for purchasing the solution, thus offering valuable information to the Prime salesperson and another opportunity to influence the final decision.

As with expectations about solution outcome, it is our job to ensure that timing expectations are clearly defined and mutually understood and that they are reasonable and attainable.

Defining the Decision Criteria

Once we have helped our customers create a portrait of what "fixed" is going to look like, we need to turn our attention to how they will decide on the best solution alternative available to them. To do this, we create decision criteria that offer set guidelines by which customers judge all solutions and the proof points needed to measure, analyze, and compare solution alternatives. This is where we teach the questions the customer needs to ask of any salesperson to help them sort through the smoke and mirrors of complex solutions and half-answered questions.

The truth is that alternatives always exist in the marketplace, and each carries differing degrees of risk. As we explained at the start of the chapter, there are no free moves for the customer. Prime salespeople use decision criteria and help customers recognize the consequences of their choices. This is very similar to the process doctors go through when prescribing medications. The FDA requires that every prescription drug carry with it a full description of contraindications, warnings, adverse reactions, possible side effects, and detailed instructions for proper dosage. Patients often ignore this "small print," but doctors use it to make informed decisions about prescribing a drug and communicating that choice to their patients.

This awareness reinforces reasonable expectations, supports a high-quality choice of solution, and serves as the basis for monitoring the progress and adjusting solutions during implementation.

Taking an active hand in the formulation of decision criteria is a task that is largely nonexistent in conventional selling. Thus, traditional salespeople are depending on their customers to provide these criteria, and, as we already know, customers typically do not have the expertise to undertake

---

Key Thought
What Can Go Wrong Will Go Wrong

The same concept that applies to medical prescriptions also applies to business solutions. To make a high-quality decision about solutions, the customer must be aware of the potential pain and risk associated with available alternatives.

this task. Further, conventional salespeople are often reluctant to admit the existence of alternative solutions that might compete with their own offerings. They are like ostriches—sticking their heads in the sand and hoping that the customer will not see anything more than they can see themselves.

Conversely, Prime professionals face the reality that the marketplace is a competitive arena and that their customers often have instant access to information about competing solutions. They know that their customers are going to explore these alternative solutions with or without them, and they understand that the only true choice salespeople have in the matter is whether to participate in that process. As always, and as we've seen throughout the Prime Process, successful salespeople recognize that the preferred alternative is to help guide and shape the customer's decision process.

Decision criteria specify the features, situations, and capabilities required to achieve the expectations of the customer. They are the material specifications of the customer's vision. They enable customers to explore treatment options in an organized fashion, ensure that alternatives are weighed equally, allow customers to match solutions to expectations, and then test and confirm their choices.

Decision criteria are *not* a laundry list of features and benefits. In other words, salespeople can't simply cut and paste the capabilities of their offerings under the heading of "Decision Criteria." The criteria must grow from the expectations of the customer, and they must be directly connected to the findings of the Diagnose phase. When we specify a solution's capability within the decision criteria, it must relate to a symptom or indicator of the problem. Otherwise, there is no defensible reason for requiring the capability in the solution.

This is a critical connection. How often have you had a customer become enamored with a competitor's product or service feature that sounds, looks, and smells good, but which the customer doesn't need? The customer is seduced by the decision principle: "If in doubt, it's better to have a feature than not have it." In this state, customers suddenly announce that they "need" a specific capability and they want to know if you have it.

For example, the feature in question is a whicker attachment (an imaginary part), which your product does not include. It is usually obvious what has happened: Another salesperson has presented the whicker as the latest and greatest product feature, and now the customer wants a whicker. How do you counter that claim and the customer's desire? The decision criteria. They tell us whether a whicker actually addresses an indicator present in the customer's problem or if it is a superfluous feature. (By the way, if the customer does actually need a whicker and we can't provide it, it may be time to be leaving.)

In complex sales, the list of decision criteria can quickly get unwieldy. We usually suggest that salespeople focus on a short list of three criteria that will have the most impact on the customer's decision. Within each of these three criteria, we need to teach our customers to ask the solution questions that make sense in our industry. We are, in essence, showing our customers how to sort through the smoke and mirrors that typify so many sales presentations and grasp the information that they need to decide among competing solutions.

For example, a customer is planning to buy capital equipment that requires authorized service and install it in plants in 21 countries around the world. Service support is obviously a critical issue in such a purchase. Typically, a customer in this situation asks: "Do you have a service program in place that includes my 21 international plants?" The salesperson replies, "Of course, we offer a global service program." The customer checks this solution criteria and moves on.

Next, the customer buys from this salesperson, and the capital equipment installed in Singapore breaks down. The customer calls for service and finds out that it will be 48 hours before the service technician in Maryland can get there. There are two days of downtime before the tech even arrives on-site, and the customer is wondering how many days of downtime will be recorded when he starts multiplying the number by 21 countries.

The global service program that the salesperson promised actually means that his company will send a tech from its headquarters to wherever the equipment is located. But the customer never discovered that because he never asked the next logical questions: "Where are your service techs located?" "How long will it take to get one of them to my sites?"

Prime sales professionals pay particular attention to those points where their product and service strengths intersect with the customer's decision criteria. Prime opportunities to differentiate ourselves from our competitors exist at these points.

An example drawn from the training industry illustrates the idea. The effectiveness of training is heavily dependent on the abilities of the person conducting the training and how well he or she understands and relates to the audience. Accordingly, the attributes of the trainer should be one of the decision criteria considered by customers.

If you were a salesperson for a training firm and your company paid particular attention to matching the experience and abilities of trainers to their clients (sending trainers to meet clients before sessions and asking the trainer to customize those sessions, for instance), you have a competitive advantage over competitors whose trainers do not meet clients before the actual training and who assign trainers by geographical location or at random based on previously scheduled work. It only makes sense that you would implant these criteria in the customer's decision process. Customers would receive a high-quality solution, and you would have a greater chance to earn their business.

As always, the ultimate goal of decision criteria is to empower our customers with the information they need to make a high-quality decision. When we have established the decision criteria that the customer will use to find the best solution to the problem, there is only one task left for the Prime salesperson: confirmation.

Confirmation and the Discussion Document

One of the biggest obstacles in complex sales is the inability of salespeople and customers to understand each other. We call this gap between the two parties the *Valley of Mystification*. The salesperson stands on one side of the valley unable to see the problem, but with the solution in hand; the customer stands on the other side experiencing the problem perhaps not understanding it completely and unable to fully understand the solution. As a result, a successful sale becomes a random collision of pain, product, and lucky timing.

The process of confirmation is one way out of the valley. By confirming that our customers and we are on the same page and that everyone involved in the engagement comprehends both the problem and parameters of the solution, we eliminate ambiguity and confusion and foster mutual understanding.

In the Prime Process, confirmation is driven by a *discussion document*. Discussion documents are much like preliminary sketches that architects draw. In the process of designing a building, an architect and the client first discuss the features that the client wants in the design; then the architect draws a preliminary design based on those requirements. A client can't actually build a house from these drawings, but they do serve as a starting point for the blueprints that are needed to begin construction.

The discussion document serves a similar purpose in the complex sale. This pencil sketch recaps the problem, its financial impact, the customer's expectations, and the decision criteria with which the best solution will be determined. It sums up the engagement to this point and puts into writing the agreements and understandings reached with the customer.

When a customer won't confirm the discussion document, we know that a serious impediment to a successful sale has surfaced. Before we move forward with the engagement, we need to trace each concern or disconnect back to its source and resolve it to the customer's satisfaction.

Key Thought
What's Wrong with This Picture?

Salespeople tend to forget that there are always conflicting objectives coexisting within organizations. When the design of a solution that is clearly in the best interest of the organization is meeting resistance, you must first ask yourself, "What is wrong with this picture?" When you identify what it is that doesn't make sense, ask a second question, "Under what circumstances would this refusal to confirm make sense?"

When the customer does confirm the contents of the discussion document, it tells the salesperson two things: First, all of the requirements needed to design the best solution are addressed, and second, it is now the right time to formally offer the customer that solution. It is time to move into the final phase of the Prime Process, Delivery.

Normally, the answers to these two questions lead you to one or more members of the cast of characters who believe that they will experience pain because of the solution. You can neutralize that pain by recognizing it and addressing it in the solution or by building a consensus that it must be accepted for the overall benefit of the organization.

7

Delivering on the Prime Promise

*Keeping Close to the Customer and
Ahead of the Competition*

We hear two common statements from executives when they call on us to help them improve their organization's sales performance. They sound like this: "Our team isn't bringing home the sale often enough. We can't overcome objections and close." "We're getting beat up on price. We don't know how to negotiate." Can you see what's right and what's wrong in these statements?

Here's how we interpret the situation: The statement of the problem—declining sales and profit ratios—is based on observations and represents a very real and serious situation. But the identification of the cause—the inability of salespeople to close and negotiate—is an opinion and, in fact, is not the actual cause of the problem.

Closing and negotiation skills, in the traditional sense, are rarely needed in the complex sale. Or, more accurately, you don't need to worry about closing and negotiation during the eleventh hour if you follow the Prime Process. These two most erroneous, and often feared, tasks in sales are simply no longer necessary.

This is a difficult idea for salespeople to grasp. "What? No objections?" "No negotiations?" Their incredulity is a measure of how deeply the conventional selling mind-set is implanted in the psyche of the salesforce and how radical a shift away from that mind-set the Prime Process actually represents.

The Prime Process eliminates the dependency on closing and negotiation skills because by the time the complex sale comes to its conclusion, our customers have already understood and confirmed the causes of their problems, the consequences of those problems, the parameters of a high-quality solution, and the financial value of that solution. As long as our offerings address these preestablished elements, all of our customers' concerns have been met. There is literally nothing for our customers to object to and no reason to question the price of our products and services. If any unexpected questions do surface, they can simply be linked back to the information that we've already developed and confirmed with the customer.

Negotiation takes on a new definition in the Prime Process. The essence of the Prime Process is clear and precise communication and collaboration—a continual "mutual understanding." Continual mutual understanding and agreement is negotiation at its finest. *Open collaboration from moment one* of the process means the process proceeds with continual agreement. If the Prime salesperson is still engaged with the customer by the time the Delivery phase is reached, he or she has already passed all the milestones required to provide the solution. We should not be in the room unless both parties believe there is a strong fit between their problems and our solutions. This translates to no objections, no price negotiations and pressure, and no buyer's remorse or other deal-canceling reactions. It also means faster sales cycles, more predictable outcomes, and higher margin transactions—all of those things that define success in careers and organizations.

So, what are we doing at the conclusion of the Prime Process? The final phase of the process, *Delivery*, is focused on two goals: (1) successful completion of the sale and (2) the postsale relationship between the salesperson, the organization, and the customer.

Elements of the first goal, successful completion, include formalizing the sale and then delivering and implementing the solution. Formalizing the sale includes the salesperson's preparation and presentation of the proposal and the customer's acceptance thereof. In delivery and implementation of solutions, salespeople manage the risks of

---

Key Thought
Would You Do What You Are about to
Propose to Your Customer?

Before you enter the Delivery phase, there is one question to ask yourself: If you were the customer, knowing what you know, would you do what you are about to propose? This is the acid test of the sales professional and the primary tenet of ethical selling. Imagine that the customer is your best friend or that you are the doctor and the customer is your patient. Would you be offering the same solution? If not, now is the time to stop the process and reconsider the alternatives.

---

the solution implementation and ensure that their customers are getting what they have been promised.

The second goal of the Delivery phase is focused on the postsale relationship between the salesperson, the organization, and the customer. It includes, first, the monitoring, correction (if necessary), and communication of solution outcomes; and second, the expansion of the business relationship salespeople have been building throughout the Prime Process. We call salespeople who successfully establish this expanded role *Prime Resources* because they have become the preferred providers for their products and services in their customers' minds.

Formalizing the Sale

The first thing we deliver in the final phase of the Prime Process is the proposal. The proposal is a formal, polished version of the discussion document that we prepared at the end of the Design phase. It is the complete story of the best solution to the customer's problem—what that solution is and how we arrived at it.

The proposal lays out all of the technical specifications of the solution and the contractual details that go into a binding agreement. And, like the discussion document, the proposal summarizes all the findings we have developed thus far in the Prime Process. It leads the customer step-by-step back over the bridge to change from the solution itself to the decision criteria and outcome expectations to the problem indicators and consequences. This articulation and summary of the chain of decisions also takes into consideration and addresses the critical perspectives of each member of the cast of characters.

The proposal in the Prime Process is an instrument of confirmation. It is a formal statement of everything that has already been agreed on. It should contain no new information; it should inspire no debate. It is only the formal closing of the sale.

Key Thought
No Surprises

Lawyers are taught never to ask a witness a question unless they already know how the witness is going to answer. The same advice holds true for proposals in the complex sale: Never put anything in the proposal that the customer has not already agreed to and confirmed. When we surprise our customers with new information in proposals, they will surely surprise us with unexpected, and usually negative, responses.

When we use the word *confirmation* to describe a proposal in the Prime Process, we are making an important distinction between it and the typical sales proposal. In conventional sales, the proposal is used as an instrument of *consideration*. In other words, it is presented to customers so that they may analyze and judge the solution being proposed. That is why the content of most sales proposals is devoted almost exclusively (usually 90 percent or more) to the solution being offered.

Proposals devoted to solutions do not tell the full story of the engagement. They don't explain the customer's problem or why the solution proposed is in the customer's best interest. As a result, they are incomplete and unconvincing and serve mainly to generate objections. The conventional solution-focused proposal is full of pitfalls.

Further, as we discussed earlier in this book, proposals based almost entirely on the salesperson's offering are largely a waste of time. They all sound alike to the customer, who can't connect their features and benefits to a well-defined problem. Therefore, they unerringly lead customers to decisions based on the lowest common denominator, the price. (They also inhibit the salesperson's ability to differentiate his or her company and offerings.)

Effective proposal writing in complex sales is part art and part science, and it is a topic unto itself. Tom Sant's book, *Persuasive Business Proposals*, provides a great guide.[1] We now provide a few tips specifically for practitioners of the Prime Process.

Write for the Invisible Decision Maker

Recently, we analyzed a proposal prepared by an outsourcing company in the commercial insurance industry. The company was offering to take over control of the management of all of its client's insurance needs, and the client represented a large account, almost 10 times the size of the company's average customer. The service being offered was complex; the proposal, on the other hand, was two pages long. The first page specified the rates per $100 in salary by the job classifications of the client's employees. The second page specified a rebate that would be earned if the client's incurred loss ratio remained below certain levels. That was the entire proposal. Picture yourself as a senior executive at the prospective client who hasn't been part of the engagement to this point but is being asked to approve this sale. Would you green light this expenditure? On what grounds?

Proposals need to be written for the invisible decision maker. Not because there always is one, but because proposals need to tell the entire story of the engagement convincingly and coherently. When we keep this imaginary reader in our minds as we prepare the proposal, we have a constant sounding board for the content. It can guide us to a proposal that is a business report—one that explains a problem, the parameters of a solution, and the solution itself.

Echo the Customer's Voice

When we meet with clients who are interested in our services, we tape the conversations whenever possible and take copious notes when we can't tape. There is no ulterior motive here; we aren't trying to trip up or trap customers. What we are doing is trying to capture the voice of the customer.

All organizations have their own language. There are special phrases and meanings that make sense to and strike chords in the people at work within them. Listen for key phrases and adopt them. Echo this language in your proposal. Customers should not be able to distinguish the proposal from an internal report prepared by someone in their own company.

Enlist the Cast of Characters

The cast of characters is the salesperson's primary source of information throughout the Prime Process. When the time comes to present the proposal, we can enlist their help once more by asking members of the cast to present selected portions of the proposal themselves.

We can call on them during the presentation, saying, for example, "Bill, this information on page 10 grew out of our discussions. Maybe you want to walk us through it." Hearing a colleague present sends a powerful message of support for the proposal and confirmation for the solution to the rest of the decision team.

"Go for the No" One More Time

When our customers indicate their acceptance of the proposal, it is time to "go for the no" once more. Throughout the Prime Process, we have indicated our readiness to walk away from the engagement any time that the customer decides that there is no good reason to continue.

What would you say to a friend who has told you that he has made a major decision? You would probably ask, "Are you sure?" We establish ourselves as "best friend" one more time when we ask customers questions such as "Are you sure this solution fulfills your needs? Did we miss anything?" Further, if the customer is not sure about the decision, we find out on the spot (not three days later) and have the opportunity to allay any doubts that still exist.

Delivering the Solution

What does the conventional salesperson do after the sale is closed? Move on to the next victim. That sounds harsh, but unfortunately, that is exactly how many customers believe salespeople behave. Prime salespeople deal with this prejudice by breaking type once again and remaining conspicuously involved in the delivery and implementation of solutions.

Our involvement in the delivery of the solution grows out of a simple idea: *A single order does not make a relationship.* Relationships are built on dependability and the customers' ability and willingness to rely on our expertise whenever they need assistance. When salespeople hand off customers and move on to new customers, no matter how smooth and problem-free the process, customers are going to perceive this as an abandonment of the relationship.

We are not saying that salespeople should spend all of their time with existing customers. Obviously, a major part of a salesperson's job is to discover, engage, and establish new accounts. But too often, salespeople move on too quickly. We need to recognize the value of existing customers and devote a significant portion of our time to the retention and expansion of our relationships with those customers. This value is well documented. A study by Bain & Company calculated that in the insurance industry, a 5 percent increase in retention results in a 60 percent jump in profits; in employer services, a 4 percent increase in retention results in a 21 percent jump in profits; and in banking, a 5 percent increase in retention results in a 40 percent increase in profits.[2] When salespeople stay directly involved with customers during and after the delivery of the solution, they capture a sizable opportunity.

The same cooperative and diagnostic skills that carried us through the previous phases of the Prime Process are put to work in the physical delivery of the solution. Prime salespeople start this work by confronting and communicating the implementation problems that their customers regularly encounter. If your company never has implementation problems, this doesn't apply. However, in our experience, that is rarely the case. We find that the typical solution implementation and a customer's reaction to it look something like Figure 7.1.

Typically, salespeople gloss over the ups and downs of implementation. Perhaps hoping that problems will not occur, they try to ignore them. Thus, when problems do pop up, customers are not anticipating them and are caught by surprise, maximizing their dissatisfaction. This, in

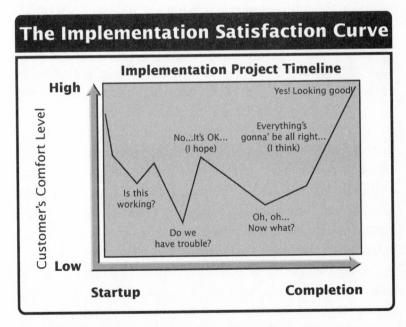

FIGURE 7.1 Implementation Satisfaction Curve

turn, forces the salesperson and the service and support staff to spend too much time in damage control and recovery, or risk a worse reaction from the unhappy customer.

One way in which this negative cycle can be avoided is by analyzing the problems and negative reactions that tend to surface in delivery and defuse them before their occurrence. For example, when we first started teaching the Prime Process, we found that it elicited strong, defensive feelings from a small percentage of salespeople who felt extremely threatened by the idea of changing their business-as-usual mind-sets. The reaction of this group was to attack—they would corner their managers and complain that our ideas were impossible to execute and it was sheer insanity to even consider adopting them. This caused managers to start questioning the effectiveness of the program and come to us for help.

We, of course, practiced what we preached and diagnosed the negative reactions. When we did, we discovered that the complaints were almost exclusively coming from the lowest ranks of the salesforce. Surprisingly, those who needed the most help were resisting it the most. Since then, we prepare managers by telling them to expect to hear a small number of participants attack our concepts, we predict that those complainers will likely be among their least effective performers, and we give them a script with which to handle the problem. The managers still hear a few complaints, but they handle them with ease. Thus, an implementation problem is defused before it occurs, and we are reaffirming our expert status in the customer's mind.

Defusing potential problems before they occur is an excellent, practical solution to delivery snafus, but we also recognize that salespeople won't be able to anticipate every implementation problem. Another way to break the negative cycle that begins when customers are unpleasantly surprised

---

Key Thought
You Must Be Prepared to Not Be Prepared

Like pilots who are trained to react to emergencies, almost reflexively and without panic, Prime sales professionals also need to be prepared to not be prepared. They must be so prepared, that their response seems natural and spontaneous. They remain cool, calm, and collected when confronted by upset customers. They say, "I'm sorry to hear that. That doesn't sound good." They then move immediately into diagnosis, "When you say it doesn't work, help me understand—walk me through it."

---

during implementation is to adopt a mind-set that admits the possibility of problems and prepares you to address them.

The fact that customers experience problems in the implementation of a solution is often less of an issue than how salespeople respond. Prime salespeople prepare for these problems by understanding that they do occur, providing the customer with the means to report those problems, and, most importantly, by reacting to reported problems in a cooperative manner by acting as a business partner and diagnostician.

Measuring and Reporting Results— Value Achieved

After the solution has been delivered and implemented, salespeople have one final task. The last step in the Delivery phase and the end of the Prime Process itself is the measurement and reporting of the results generated by the solution.

Of all the sales methodologies, the Prime Process best positions salespeople to measure and report results. We have already determined the indicators of the problem, its financial impact, and expectations of the solution and its value. In delivery, we simply turn back to these figures, measure them against the actual results, and report our findings to the customer.

If the expected outcomes have not been achieved, we prove our value and professionalism to the customer once again by diagnosing the obstacles that are holding them back and designing new solutions. If the expected outcomes are being achieved, we can use the results report to open new business opportunities with the customer.

Salespeople should complete this work because of the following three compelling reasons:

1. It ensures that the promised outcomes have been achieved. Salespeople may be able to succeed in the short term by closing sales and moving on to new customers, but to succeed in the long term, we must deliver on our promises.

2. It provides the basis for renewing the Prime Process. We call our sales methodology a process, but it is also a cycle. When our customers achieve or exceed the outcomes they envisioned for the solution, we can renew the Prime Process by using their results to move back into the diagnostic mode and then design new solutions that are capable of providing improved results.

3. It allows us to establish our position as one of our customer's preferred resources, which maximizes the

long-term profitability of the customer relationship and erects intimidating barriers for our competitors to overcome.

The ultimate goal is to become our customer's Prime Resource for the solutions we bring to market. This relationship sets us apart from the competition in the customer's mind and leads to an ongoing role of diagnostic problem solver. Again, a source of business advantage.

Here are five characteristics of Prime Resources:

1. Prime Resources are active participants in their customers' businesses. They understand those businesses and take an active role in their success.

2. Prime Resources commit to long-term growth relationships with their customers. They allocate the time and energy needed to work with their customers on a regular basis.

3. Prime Resources base their recommendations on measurable problems and outcomes. They are always working from the reality of the customer's world.

4. Prime Resources act as early warning systems for customers. They surface unexposed problems and notify customers of changes in products, technologies, and markets that may impact their businesses.

5. Prime Resources stay close. They know that two-thirds of customers stop doing business with companies because they feel unappreciated, neglected, or treated indifferently.[3]

If it sounds as though there is a good deal of work involved in becoming a Prime Resource, there is. At least, there is more work than the conventional salesperson typically undertakes. But the rewards are exponentially higher.

In the "You snooze, you lose" world of business, Prime salespeople are always awake and alert to significant changes in the environment. Their customers learn to depend on this alertness and become loyal, long-term customers.

Further, in sales, your best customer is always your competitor's best prospect. The customers of Prime salespeople, however, have a much higher resistance level than the average customer. Our customers know the value that they derive from the Prime relationship. So, when competitors call them and say, "We can give you the same thing for 10 to 20 percent less," our customers don't get stars in their eyes. They know the right questions to ask and the traps to avoid. They are also well aware of all of the decisions that go into choosing a high-quality solution—after all, that is exactly what we have taught them in the Prime Process.

Prime Performance Leadership

Leading Professionals in the Complex Sale

Sales managers have one of the toughest jobs in the organization, and frequently they're given few tools and little development support with which to do their job. Sales executives have much in common with managers in professional sports. Their records are posted for all to see; their jobs are secure—as long as they are winning and their success is dependent on the performance of their teams.

Plenty of coaches have enjoyed short-term success. Maybe a dream team comes along or the competition falls apart or perhaps the planets line up just right for one season. But long-term winners—legendary leaders such as Vince Lombardi and Don Shula in football, Phil Jackson in basketball, and Roger Penske in auto racing—don't rely on luck. They build sports dynasties by imposing systems on their organizations, recruiting and coaching players who are capable of executing them, and running those systems with exceptional discipline day in and day out.

Joe Gibbs, the first person to ever lead championship teams in both professional football and NASCAR auto racing, says, "A win at any track doesn't just happen by accident. We don't simply fill our cars with gas, crank them up, and hope we can drive faster or outlast our opponents. Every detail of the race is thought through, including contingency plans and backup parts. We have a game plan for the race and we attempt to follow it as closely as possible."[1] Like great coaches, sales executives need a winning game plan.

Unhappily, many executives are content to approach sales as a numbers game. If they aren't generating the performance results they need, they don't reexamine the selling system (if one is in place). They simply step on the gas and try to do more of what they are already doing. They ask their teams to work harder instead of smarter. We've already discussed why this strategy doesn't work in the complex sale, but there is one more consideration that bears mentioning: When managers run the sales function as a numbers game, they are depending almost exclusively on the innate talents of individual salespeople—and that virtually guarantees mediocre results.

This is a function of the Pareto Principle, the "80/20 Rule," which, when extended to sales performance, suggests that 20 percent of the salesforce develops 80 percent of sales. If you turn that ratio on its head, it tells us that 80 percent of salespeople are struggling just to keep their heads above water. These figures were born out of a 10-year study of 18,000 salespeople conducted by the Caliper Research Organization, which found that 55 percent should not be in sales at all, 25 percent were in the wrong kind of sales, and only 20 percent were properly placed.[2]

The myth of the Pareto Principle is that it is somehow set in stone and that we must accept these results. In fact, those results are simply part of the numbers game. It may be impractical to attempt to build a salesforce composed entirely of "20 percenters," but there is no reason that you can't double the number of top performers in your organization and substantially boost your sales revenue. You should be able to transform underperformers into full-fledged producers, and in those instances where you can't, leave them behind for your competitors to hire. It is all a matter of adopting a systematic approach to complex sales (see Figure 8.1).

Systems are certainly not a foreign concept in professional and business disciplines. No one would suggest that airlines allow pilots to fly planes any way they wish or that hospitals allow surgeons to operate on patients however they please. Manufacturers don't allow workers to run production lines any way they see fit. They all work within preestablished systems. Likewise, a business needs a sales

"We only hire experienced professionals."
Translation: We don't have a system for developing successful salespeople.

"The salesforce is made of creative and independent individuals."
Translation: We can't control them.

"It takes six to nine months to learn our business."
Translation: It will be at least a year before we can judge their productivity.

"They've got some good irons in the fire."
Translation: There's lots of smoke, but we have no idea how the sales engagements are progressing.

"You just can't find good people anymore."
Translation: We don't know where to look or what to look for.

FIGURE 8.1   The Top Five Excuses for Sales as Usual

system. It needs a selling system that is capable of leveraging the full potential of salespeople and the sales team; enables it to track, manage, and continuously improve the entire sales process; and coordinate the efforts of all of the different functions involved in managing complex relationships and successfully completing complex transactions. For all the reasons we discussed in previous chapters, we believe that the system must be decision-focused and diagnosis-based—a Prime Process.

Now, the question is how to create a decision process based on your products and services and hire and develop a salesforce capable of executing that process.

Structuring Your Prime Process

The Prime Process is a metamodel for the successful execution of complex sales, but to turn it into a more detailed blueprint, it must be customized according to the unique value proposition and offerings your company brings to market. We talked about how this work can be accomplished at the level of the individual salesperson, but to begin to realize the full potential of the process, it needs to be distributed over the entire sales, marketing, and support organization.

All four phases of the Prime Process must be aligned to your unique situation, but most organizations also find that there are specific phases of the Diagnostic Business Development process that are particularly important in their selling system. When you identify and focus on these areas, you will have honed in on the place in which your customers typically require the most assistance and in which you can leverage your ability to differentiate your company from your competitors.

You can use the simple matrix in Figure 8.2 to identify your focal point in the Prime Process.

We assume that none of you fall into the lower left quadrant, because if the complexity of the problems you address and the solutions you offer are both low, you do not have a complex sale after all. If you do fall into that quadrant, you need to verify your finding, and if it is confirmed, start exploring whether you should maintain a salesforce. A Web site, direct mail, or some other self-serve model, such as that used in office supplies businesses like Staples and OfficeMax, is more efficient and cost effective in the simple problem/simple solution scenario.

It is normal to have different parts of your business fall into different parts of the matrix. One of our clients provides automated document storage and retrieval systems and distributes them through Staples and OfficeMax. Their solutions range from literally the paper file folder to a sophisticated document imaging system.

Moving clockwise around the matrix, when the complexity of our customers' problems increases, but the complexity of the solution remains low, the Diagnosis phase becomes the most critical aspect of the Prime Process. As problems become increasingly complex, the customer's ability to identify and understand those problems decreases. Thus, salespeople must pay particular attention to the work of diagnosis. (By the way, when diagnosis is critical to the customer's success, you might want to consider charging for the service, as in a consulting/professional services business model.)

In the upper right-hand quadrant of the matrix, both problems and solutions are complex, and we would place special emphasis on the Design phase of the Prime Process. When problems and solutions are complex, customers find it difficult to connect the two. Thus, the solution designer's

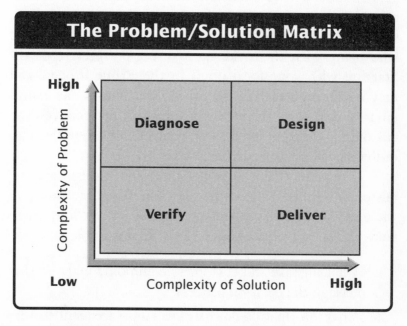

FIGURE 8.2 The Problem/Solution Matrix

ability to align the problem to the best solution becomes a paramount concern.

Finally, in the lower right-hand corner of the matrix, the solution is complex, but the problem is not. When this is the case, you should put special emphasis on the Delivery phase of the Prime Process. With complex solutions, you need to concentrate on implementation, execution, and results measurement. (When Delivery is critical to the customer's success, you might consider charging a fee for that work, as in a professional services business model.)

The quadrant that best represents your business is a good place to begin analyzing and customizing the decision process that you will bring to your customers. Typically, organizations create a cross-functional team to undertake this work. This business development team usually includes representatives of each function directly involved in the sales process—marketing, sales, service, and support. It should also include representatives from other internal functions, such as product development and finance, and customers who bring with them the most direct perspective of all. Starting with your focal point in the Prime Process and moving through each of the other three phases, the team's job is to customize the process from three perspectives: the customer's decision needs, our competitive strengths, and our competitor's competitive strengths.

To ensure that you understand and incorporate the customer's decision needs in the customized process, you want the business development team to answer four questions about each of the phases in the Prime Process:

1. What mistakes do customers commonly make in this phase of the decision process?
2. What information do customers most frequently overlook or not consider in this phase?

3. What are the most difficult things for customers to understand in this phase?

4. What level of professional education or experience is required to understand this phase?

As the team members move from phase to phase, they need to be sure to consider each of the major decision elements in the phases of the process. Thus, in Diagnosis, they consider the analysis of the problem, its consequences, and prioritization. In Design, they consider the expected solution outcomes, the alternative approaches, the investment parameters, and the decision criteria. In Delivery, they consider implementation issues and measurement of solution outcomes. And, even though Discovery does not have a place on the matrix, the team can ask each of the four questions in terms of the optimal strategy for the initial contact (because this is the first place the customer is directly involved).

Once the team has examined and customized the Prime Process from the customer's perspective, it is time to turn the focus inward and ensure that competitive strengths of your organization and your offerings are incorporated into the process. For instance, in the Diagnose phase, the team would ensure that the process enables the salesforce to diagnose early and often for the indicators that your offerings address most decisively. That way, the salesforce can size up prospects and forecast its chances of winning the sale more efficiently and accurately. A forecast based on the customer's decision that indicators are present and that the dollar impact of the problem is significant, is more accurate than a forecast based on the salesperson recognizing the customer's "interest" in the solution. In Design, they would emphasize those areas where the competitive strengths of your offerings are a close match with the customer's solution outcomes and decision criteria.

When the team has explored the Prime Process from the perspective of your competitive strengths, the members should make a final pass through the phases. This time, they want to customize the process in terms of your organization's competitors. The goal here is to enable the salesforce to identify those situations—that is, the physical indicators, the solution expectations, and the measurable outcomes—in which the competition has a strong advantage. This information allows us to predict the outcome early in the sales process with greater accuracy.

Hiring the Prime Salesperson

Perhaps more than any other profession in business, the sales profession is thought to be personality driven. Many people speak of the "born salesperson" as if the ability to sell is genetic. Organizations implicitly subscribe to this view when they attempt to staff their salesforces by identifying and hiring people who exhibit the personality traits of the legendary born salesperson.

Are there people who are naturally better suited to selling? Sure, some individuals are brought up in an environment that enhances their communication skills and goal orientation and possess an aptitude that later is described as "born" into the profession. But how many? And, are they available? When a company's sole strategy for success is to hire a bunch, turn them loose, and hope there are a few born salespeople in the mix who can work their magic, it is playing the numbers game and it is going to get Pareto Principle results.

Why do sales managers keep hiring salespeople based on personality? Because without a systematic method of determining the true ingredients of sales success, they have little choice but to attribute it to some random genetic permutation.

The reality is that successful professionals in other disciplines, such as doctors, lawyers, and pilots, do not exhibit a single personality, and neither do successful sales professionals. A good selling system allows multiple personality types to be successful and helps us move beyond the stereotypical salesperson, the aggressive, outgoing James Bond type. With a Prime system in place, we can free ourselves from the personality-driven sales syndrome.

What kind of sales candidates do we want? Obviously, we need people who can fulfill the role of a complex sales professional—that is, people who can execute the system, learn and use the skills, and live the discipline.

Assessment instruments remain the best way to quickly and accurately predict the performance of sales candidates. With that said, we need to be sure to carefully explore what the assessments we use actually measure. The vast majority of assessment instruments are one-dimensional, and they are aimed at identifying a conventional sales personality. This type of instrument identifies the James Bond-style salesperson for you, but that profile is appropriate only for simple sales (and perhaps not even that). It does not pinpoint superior performers in a complex sales environment. In fact, if you run most top performers through a standard sales profiling tool, they will likely be rejected: They aren't aggressive enough, will take "no" for answer, won't close.

To identify Prime sales candidates, we combine three assessments to create a holistic profile of the candidate and offer a high probability of predicting the success of an individual working in complex sales:

1. A behavioral assessment that offers insight into a candidate's behavior style. This is the "how" of their behavior.[3] We are looking for candidates who portray the

behavior style of the doctor, the best friend, and the detective.

2. An assessment that identifies the candidate's personal interests and values, which tells us "why" a candidate will sell. We are trying to understand the candidate's attitudes and motivations, and we are looking for the proverbial self-starter with a history of setting and achieving goals.

3. An assessment that provides insights into "what" the candidate can and will do relating to executing the Diagnostic Business Development process. This instrument provides an insight into the candidate's mental and emotional stamina. When the rubber hits the road, does the candidate have the intestinal fortitude and mental strength needed to actually execute the system? We also gain insights into the professional growth potential of candidates and the type of development that may be most helpful to maximize their growth potential. We're also attempting to predict if this candidate will ask the tough questions in a sale and if the candidate has the mental strength not to get emotionally involved—like a doctor calmly performing triage in a battle zone or a pilot coolly reacting to a wind shear.

Quick-Starting the Prime Sales Professional

Once you hire a candidate to work in a complex sales environment, it is your responsibility to provide the knowledge that person needs to do the job. The problem in the complex sales world is that sales training is generally relegated to product knowledge. Customer, market knowledge, and the integration of systems, skills, and discipline of the profession are largely ignored.

Typically, we find that 90 percent of sales training is devoted to the products and services being sold, and almost all of the remaining 10 percent is spent on conventional selling techniques such as prospecting, cold-calling, presentation, and closing skills. The amount of training that is devoted to understanding the customer, market knowledge, and the integration of skills that complex salespeople need to diagnose customer problems, design solutions, and deliver results is negligible, at best.

What is needed is an educational mix that more closely mirrors the medical profession. Seventy percent of the training that doctors receive is focused on diagnosis, and the remaining 30 percent is evenly split between learning about the human body (product knowledge) and learning about treatment alternatives (solutions). Companies in complex sales would do well to emulate that learning mix (see Figure 8.3).

In complex sales, we can divide optimal sales education into three categories: (1) Product Knowledge, the study of the features and benefits of the products and services you offer and how they impact the business drivers of the customer; (2) Diagnostics, the study of the customer's business, job responsibilities and the skills needed to uncover the problems customers are experiencing; and, (3) Solutions, the study of how to solve customer problems and how our products and services relate to those solutions.

How does your current sales training relate to these categories?

What percentage of your training falls into each?

Product Knowledge   _____%

Diagnostics   _____%

Solutions   _____%

FIGURE 8.3   **Sales Training Self-Assessment**

"Well begun is half done" goes the proverb; and in complex sales, that means that we need to provide new salespeople (and existing salespeople who are required to adopt a new system) with a foundation on which they can build a successful career.[4] This education not only ensures that salespeople have the tools they need, but it also serves as an appraisal structure that enables management to appraise, correct, and improve their performance.

The initial body of professional knowledge that salespeople require corresponds to the Prime Process. We need to prepare them to *Discover* new customers, *Diagnose* their problems, and *Design* and *Deliver* the solutions. To cover this ground, we typically recommend the 12-Stage Success Plan.

12-Stage Success Plan

The 12-Stage Success Plan is an on-the-job learning sequence that runs from 12 weeks to 12 months, depending on the complexity of problems they solve, the solutions our clients undertake, and the capabilities of the salesperson.

The basics of a good professional development plan start with a format based on experiential learning. Learning by doing is the most effective form of education. A good program should be hands-on, sequential in nature, and incorporate a learning process that builds in complexity as the salesperson's knowledge and confidence grow.

Effective learning should also include scheduled milestones, at least one for each stage, during which salespeople must demonstrate their proficiency before they can move ahead. (In our programs, new salespeople sign personal development agreements before they are hired acknowledging that failure to meet the milestones is grounds for termination.) One vital dimension of these milestones is the feedback the learner receives. Learners need to receive objective, consistent, and specific feedback. Oral and written reports and presentations, travel with best-practice performers, coaching sessions, and observation of prospect and customer interviews all offer the opportunity for many people in your company to be involved in the development process and create feedback loops to ensure and enhance the transfer of knowledge.

We must consider the decision to hire as singular and complete, based on the information available at the time of the decision. We must treat the decision to retain as a separate decision that will be based on new information received and observations made after the individual begins working with us. The point is, you can base your decision to retain on observed behavior long before you can see results in a complex sale.

The key to the effectiveness of the 12-stage plan is that at each stage of learning, a measurable and objective proof of learning is to be achieved. We must not advance the learner unless and until that proof is received. It's no different than the 12 grades of elementary and secondary education. You don't advance the student to the next grade until they have given evidence of learning the content of their current grade. Passing them will not cause the learning to happen later. It more likely means they will have to perform, minus certain skills and knowledge for quite some time.

We talk about the stages of the development program in terms of the questions each is designed to answer in the learner's mind. Learners develop the answers to these questions through both internal and external sources. Internally, they use company data and information, as well as interviews and coaching sessions with fellow salespeople and colleagues from other functions within the company.

Externally, they use industry and customer data, as well as interviews with prospective and existing customers.

We explore the 12 stages of a generic quick-start professional development program in the following paragraphs:

1. What Is Our Company All About?

Sales professionals need to know your company's history, the key people and positions, its market position, its value proposition, as well as the details of employment such as the compensation plan, expense policies, and so forth. The culminating milestone of this stage would be 2-, 5-, 10-, and 20-minute presentations (ideally video or, at least, audiorecorded) to colleagues or managers that demonstrate the new salesperson's ability to organize and present information and to give a clear picture of your company and its capabilities to a prospective customer.

2. Who Are the Customers We Serve?

In this stage, learners meet customers via the telephone and face-to-face appointments in the field. They learn who buys from your company and, more importantly, why they buy, how they perceive your company, and how satisfied they have been with the value created by your company. We want our sales professionals to learn how our customers think, how they see their businesses, what issues they face, and what market trends they see. The milestone is the salesperson's ability to create external and internal profiles for use in qualifying potential business.

3. How Do We Develop New Business?

After salespeople learn to prepare customer profiles, they need to understand the opportunity management process. In this stage, they establish an opportunity management system that enables them to coordinate their activities and set priorities. They create a plan for time and territory management based on the optimal ratio of lead types. The milestone is an internal presentation of the plan, which targets and qualifies a preagreed number of business opportunities.

4. What Is Our Diagnostic Engagement Protocol?

In this stage, salespeople learn the basics of building a diagnostic engagement strategy from a prospect's profile. The diagnostic prospecting and qualifying protocol is the engagement strategy for a prospective customer. It details the Discovery process, the cast of characters, the areas to be diagnosed, the best kinds of questions for finding the answers needed, and the diagnostic process the salesperson will complete. The milestone is an internal, simulated exercise in which the salesperson prepares and engages in a typical first call and other strategic diagnostic situations.

5. What Is Your Personal Business Plan?

In this stage, salespeople develop an initial version of an individualized business plan that includes their financial goals and specifies the quality and quantity of activities required to achieve those goals and the internal/external resources needed to help support those goals. As described in Chapter 4, a personal business plan is a subset of the regional, national, and corporate business plans. The milestone is a review of the proposed plan and, on approval, the commitment to meet those goals.

6. What Are Our Solutions?

Product and service training does not appear until the middle of the program to ensure that salespeople understand customers and the problems those customers face before they begin to learn about the solutions you offer. In this stage, salespeople learn much more than the technical features and benefits of your offerings. They learn how to diagnose the indicators present in the absence of those features and specific departments and job responsibilities in the customer's business in which to look for them. They also learn how to connect solutions to customers' business drivers. The milestone is a presentation along with an internal role-playing simulation in which the salesperson moves from problem diagnosis to solution design. Periodic audio/videotaping of the salesperson's presentations allows for self-critique and provides auditory/visual baselines of performance.

7. Can You Now Develop Business?

During this stage, salespeople begin applying their knowledge in the field. They prepare for and initiate new engagements, set qualified diagnostic appointments, and follow up on leads received. They remain closely supervised and are coached as necessary. The milestone is the ability to "get invited in" by new customers and initiate a constructive engagement.

8. Can You Diagnose the Customer's Situation?

In this stage, salespeople conduct customer calls with an observer. They plan account strategy and prepare for and conduct diagnostic calls. At the conclusion of each call, they receive immediate feedback from their observer and incorporate new learning as it occurs. Milestones are the ability to diagnose symptoms and causes of problems, as well as establish a mutual understanding of the diagnosis with various individuals in the customer's cast of characters.

9. Can You Determine the Cost of the Problem?

In this stage, salespeople extend the work of diagnosis to the establishment of problem consequences and the calculation of the problem's financial impact. Salespeople demonstrate their understanding of the three elements of total cost (direct, indirect, and lost opportunity) and the formulas of cost calculation to sales managers, and then in the field with customers. An observer offers feedback at the conclusion of each call, and the milestone is the proven ability to move an engagement into the Design phase.

10. Are You Perceived as a Creative Problem Solver By Your Customers?

In this stage, salespeople learn and demonstrate the skills of solution design. They link and discuss solution options in terms of the problem, its total cost, the client's expectations for change, and the investment customers are willing to make to achieve their expected outcomes. This knowledge is acquired first in internal interviews, classes, and role plays. Then, an internal presentation is made, and, finally, the knowledge is demonstrated during supervised calls on customers. The milestone is the ability to help the customer establish desired outcomes, create an optimal solution, and align selection criteria with the solution that will be proposed.

11. Can You Propose an Effective Solution?

In this stage, salespeople learn and demonstrate their ability to translate the customer's expectations into a compelling solution. They create a discussion document, gain confirmation, and translate that discussion document into a formal

---

Reality Check
Is Your Company Creating General
Practitioners or Specialists?

The complex sale requires salespeople who are experts in the problems their customers face and their solutions. Yet, we often find that salespeople in complex environments are stretched too thin. They are responsible for either calling on too broad a range of customers or offering too broad a range of products and services. In the former case, salespeople's ability to diagnose customers' problems is negatively impacted; in the latter, their ability to design and deliver solutions is negatively affected. Depth of knowledge is a key characteristic in Prime salespeople, and that requires focus on both the customer segments they serve and the range of offerings they bring to market.

---

proposal. Again, the learning is conducted in workshops, internal interviews, and in the field with an observer who offers immediate feedback. The milestone is the demonstrated ability to produce a balanced, comprehensive proposal.

12. Can You Effectively Present a Proposal?

The final stage of a quick-start training program is demonstrating the knowledge required to review the proposal with the customer and complete the customer's decision process. Again, workshops, internal interviews, role plays, and supervised calls are used until the salesperson has demonstrated the ability to successfully write new business. The milestone is the concluded sale.

A quick-start training program should conclude with the salesperson's revision of the individual business plan. This plan should now cover the next two quarters and include business and professional development goals; market, territory, and key customer analyses; targeted prospects; performance metrics; and resources needed to help achieve the goals. It should be a formal document agreed to by the salesperson and management. This business plan serves as a basis for performance monitoring, coaching, and review. These reviews should be conducted on a regular basis, weekly at first, and as the quality of the salesperson's performance improves, biweekly, then monthly, and, eventually, once per quarter. Before each review, the salesperson should write a short (one- to two-page) summary of what's working, what's not working, and what needs to be changed, if anything, to stay on goal. By having to do a self-analysis before meeting with the sales manager, development of self-management skills of the sales professional continues.

From Novice to Expert

A quick-start training program is just that—a start. The development of a Prime salesperson is a career-long quest that encompasses the continuous training, application, and refinement of a complete body of professional knowledge. The purpose of this ongoing training is the continuous improvement of a salesperson's ability to consistently operate the system, execute the skills, and adopt the disciplines of a professional. Its goal is improved closing rates, reduced proposal-to-close ratios, and the optimization of the sales process.

When salespeople successfully complete quick-start training, they have established a firm foundation for their careers. The Dreyfus Model of Skill Acquisition is a good way to understand and manage this foundation. Stuart and Richard Dreyfus, brothers and fellow professors at the University of California, created the model in the late 1970s and early 1980s. With the support of the U.S. Air Force, they studied the process of skill acquisition among aircraft pilots, racecar drivers, and chess players. (Later, additional studies by other researchers extended their findings to the nursing profession.)[5]

The Dreyfus model describes five stages of professional development: novice, advanced beginner, competent, proficient, and expert.

Novices are the new hires who do not yet know anything about business or sales. Novices must approach their new profession with an attitude of acceptance. They don't have the previous experience necessary to evaluate what they are learning; thus, they must accept the information they are offered and apply it without a complete understanding of the context in which they are working.

Advanced beginners have attained enough professional experience to begin to use their skills in a situational context. That is, they are starting to recognize aspects of situations, but they are still reacting within the guidelines of the skills themselves. These learners are not yet ready to operate without supervision.

Competent sales professionals understand all of the elements of the professional body of knowledge and can judge their responses in terms of specific situations. Professionals at this level can solve problems and efficiently organize and plan their own time. This is the point at which our 12-Stage Success Plan leaves the learner, but in contrast to what many learning theories suggest, this is not the end point in professional development.

Proficient sales professionals understand the customer's problem and its solution as a holistic process. They are incorporating their experience into their performance, and they can smoothly adapt their responses to changing situations.

Expert sales professionals represent the zenith of professional development. A good example of this is the top performing salesperson who has a seemingly casual conversation with a customer and yet leaves the meeting with a complete picture of an until-now undiscovered problem, a solution that is most likely to solve it, and strategy for moving the customer through the Prime Process. Experts *create* opportunities.

This is the greatest challenge in developing sales professionals for complex sales—to move beyond competence and develop a salesforce of experts who create value for their customers and capture an ample share of that value for their companies and themselves.

9

Prime Corporate Strategies

Translating Market Strategy into Sales Results

Business experts portray many different, and often conflicting, elements of corporate success. Some focus on innovation; others, on human capital; still others, on product and service quality. Some even focus on focus. The list goes on and a good case can usually be made for each element. But unless a company can translate its value proposition into profitable sales results, not only will the funding that all of these elements of corporate success require never materialize, but the very existence of the organization will be threatened.

The translation of value proposition into bottom-line profitability is accomplished through a go-to-market strategy that encompasses a company's market, competitive, and product strategies. Together, these elements feed into the sales strategy. Its formulation and execution is the critical work that lies at the heart of a business. The go-to-market strategy cuts across departmental functions. It directly involves the product development, marketing, sales, service, and support functions; it indirectly involves almost every other function in the business.

As with any strategy (and assuming that the resources and skills are already in place), there are four prerequisites for the successful execution of a go-to-market strategy. There must be:

1. A high level of understanding of, and agreement on, the business strategies in place to acquire, expand, and retain profitable customer relationships. Is everyone in the company united by a shared vision and a common effort?

2. A successful transfer of business strategies to departmental and individual responsibilities that encompasses both quantitative and qualitative objectives. Does everyone in the company know what they, individually and as part of a group, must accomplish to successfully achieve the defined objectives?

3. A monitoring and measurement capability that enables leadership to assess the performance of the departments and individuals as they progress toward their objectives. Can everyone monitor their progress toward the achievement of those objectives?

4. A capacity to anticipate and correct the most frequently occurring issues and obstacles blocking the successful execution of the strategy. Can everyone learn from their mistakes and respond and adapt to changing conditions?

We see many go-to market strategies fail to generate profitable results precisely because one or more of these prerequisites are ignored. For example, we encountered a company in the insurance industry that fell prey to this trap when it abruptly changed its go-to-market strategy. The company had been targeting small, blue-collar companies, such as plumbing and roofing contractors, but as the business environment changed, management decided to sell to larger, white-collar businesses. The new go-to-market strategy was delivered to the 250-member salesforce. Instead of calling on roofing contractors, they were instructed to call on medical practices, IT consultants, and law offices. Unprepared to deal with this new prospect base, the salesforce's closing ratios quickly plummeted to below 4 percent. (Interestingly, the company decided to take the traditional sales-by-numbers approach to counter poor performance. The salespeople were pressured to make more calls and give more presentations to raise their results. This is a classic example of selling harder instead of smarter.)

This example again highlights a major limitation of the conventional sales process: It offers only one response to downturns in performance—do more of what you are already doing. That response does not enable a company to address fundamental problems, gaps, and disconnects in its go-to-market strategy. Worse, as salespeople put more time and effort into a system that isn't working, they burn through valuable prospects, and the negative performance cycle is often exacerbated.

The conventional sales process is what an information technology expert would call a *legacy system*. In the computer world, legacy systems are usually outdated networks that were originally developed for limited, local purposes. As holistic, organizationally integrated networks are developed, these systems must either be modified or replaced. The conventional sales process is a legacy system in that it offers the sales department a way to communicate internally, but it doesn't connect the sales function to the rest of the organization in any meaningful way. It does not offer a common language or the filters through which sales and the other functions in the business can communicate and respond. In this sense, it contributes to the "black box" view of sales.

The black box view of sales is an attitude that we frequently find among senior executives who do not have sales experience. To them, the workings of the sales department are largely a mystery. They can set goals and send them into the black box of the salesforce, and they can tell whether those goals have been reached—after the fact. But they can't effectively manage what happens between the two points. Sales are a black box that senior management hopes will deliver the required results.

What we need is a process that can make the black box transparent—that is, capable of connecting the sales function to the rest of the organization in strategic terms and creating a common language and process through which the go-to-market strategy is formulated, executed, and monitored.

This process should also allow management to pinpoint the source of performance shortfalls. As one senior vice president in a Fortune 100 company told us, "The most frustrating things about poor sales results are not knowing where the problem originates within the organization and the finger pointing that results when you try to trace it." The Prime Process enables managers to pinpoint inefficiencies in their strategies and tactics.

Organizational Alignment and Learning

Two mechanisms must be present during the creation and execution of a go-to-market strategy. First, there must be a mechanism capable of generating strategic alignment, deployment, and results measurement within the organization. We need to ensure that everyone in the organization is speaking the same language and working in a coordinated fashion toward the realization of the plan. Second, we need a mechanism for communicating and applying the learning that is generated as our strategic plan bumps up against the realities of the marketplace.

Strategic Alignment

The division of labor into specialized tasks was, and is, a primary support in the development of the modern organization. Around the time of the American Revolution, Adam Smith glowingly described the efficiencies inherent in specialization using the example of a pin factory.[1]

Specialization, however, had a downside that Smith did not anticipate. Specialists don't always see the big picture, and different specialties often have conflicting goals.

The division of labor creates boundaries between functions, and those boundaries develop into walls. We call the divisiveness inherent in the specialization of labor the *Great Wall Syndrome,* and we often see its negative impact on the performance results of the companies with which we work. When companies suffer from the Great Wall Syndrome, the formulation and execution of strategies are segmented and isolated into functions. One department completes its work in isolation from the other functions within the company and tosses it over the wall into the next function. Each successive department does the same until the goal is achieved.[2]

In Smith's eighteenth-century pin factory, the isolation of functions was not a particularly serious matter. But in today's complex organizations, this isolation is one of the primary causes behind the failure of corporate initiatives and other change efforts. The most common results of the Great Wall Syndrome include inefficient strategy execution, inhibited communication, and slowed response times to customers and the marketplace. For instance, we've seen designers create new products with little or no input from the rest of the organization (or customers themselves); marketers create advertising campaigns and literature in a vacuum and salesforces uncover major customer needs and fail to report them.

What's missing here is the alignment of functions around the corporate value proposition. Organizations need a mechanism that can create a cohesive team, communicate and reinforce messages, get everyone working toward the same goal, and measure the progress toward that goal. Everyone in the organization should be concerned with how to create and capture value for customers. Everyone should feel a responsibility for the welfare of the customer.

One way to generate alignment around corporate goals is to require that each function involved in the formulation and execution of the go-to-market strategy cycle through the four phases of the Prime Process. The four stages of the Diagnostic Business Development process—Discover, Diagnose, Design, and Deliver—offer a single, customer-centered process through which each organizational function can explore the marketplace and ensure that their efforts are aligned with the functions.

The pharmaceutical industry is a good model of how this alignment mechanism plays out in the real world. When the R&D function of a prescription drug maker undertakes the creation of a new product, it uses a process that can be framed around the four phases of the Prime Process. R&D seeks to *Discover* a market of patients that is large enough to support the investment required to create a new drug. It *Diagnoses* the indications, causes, and consequences of patients' problems. It seeks a *Design* that will best solve the problems. And it *Delivers* the new drug through a highly regulated process of testing and government approvals.

The process is repeated as the company's marketing function and then the sales function create and align their efforts to bring the drug to the doctors and health care organizations that will prescribe it. The discovery process is used to segment and refine the markets for the drug. The indications of each segment are diagnosed, the solution design is altered to fit each, and the solution is delivered.

The doctors who prescribe the medication repeat the process yet again. They discover the profile of patients who are likely to need the drug, diagnose the individual case, design the proper dosage, and then prescribe the best solution and monitor the patient's progress throughout the delivery phase.

Each cycle of the Prime Process builds on the one before it; each is aligned with and supports the total effort. We can apply these same four phases to any product or service that grows out of a corporate value proposition. The major impact results from the accumulation of knowledge by each function and the efficient transfer of that knowledge as the product moves from development to deployment. In the absence of the Prime Process, there is a significant dilution of the ability to create and capture value as the organization moves from creating a strategy to creating results.

Organizational Learning

The second mechanism that enables the successful execution of a go-to-market strategy is the capacity to learn. MIT's Peter Senge popularized the idea of the learning organization in the early 1990s. A learning organization, he wrote, is an organization where people continually expand their capacity to create the results they truly desire, where new and expansive patterns of thinking are nurtured, where collective aspiration is set free, and where people are continually learning how to learn together.[3]

Interestingly, when Senge identified the seven learning disabilities common in today's organizations, the first was the fact that employees tend to identify with their jobs and limit their loyalty to their functional responsibilities. This identification and loyalty, said Senge, *does not* extend to the purpose and vision of the larger organization. The Great Wall Syndrome strikes again!

The problem, of course, is that when learning is stifled, so is the ability of the organization to adapt and respond to customers and, ultimately, so is profitability. Some of the largest and most successful of today's businesses were born out of the inability and/or unwillingness of existing companies to respond to the marketplace.

Intel Corporation is a notable example. In the late 1960s, Fairchild Semiconductor, which was owned by Fairchild Camera and Instrument, was one of the nation's hottest high-tech companies. Two Silicon Valley legends, general manager Robert Noyce and head of R&D, Gordon Moore, were the guiding forces behind the company's success, but their ability to respond to the fast developing market for integrated circuits was being blocked by the parent company.

"I was running the laboratory and having increasing problems trying to push product ideas through Fairchild's management before they were pursued by a half dozen start-ups around the valley," explained Moore. "It was just a good time for us both to go do something new."[4] Moore and Noyce's "something new" was Intel, a company that raised $2.5 million in startup capital in a single afternoon in July 1968 and went on to become the 800-pound gorilla of the semiconductor industry. In 2001, Intel recorded revenues of $26.5 billion; Fairchild Semiconductor's revenues were $1.4 billion. I like to call it the "two guys in a garage syndrome." The question is "Are there two guys in your organization that are feeling the need to do something in their garage to respond to your customers?"

Whether an organization must respond to new opportunities, changes in the market environment, or correct miscalculations in its own go-to-market strategy, it must have a mechanism capable of capturing and responding to feedback. It needs to be able to identify, communicate, and respond to customer needs throughout the value creation process. When the Prime Process is distributed across the organization, it can serve as that mechanism.

The Prime Process requires that the various functions within the organization charged with delivering value to customers take to the field in one voice and one process. To effectively discover, diagnose, design, and deliver, they must frame their assumptions in terms of the customer, and they must test those assumptions against the reality of the customer's world. We want the R&D professionals to view their ideas and creations through the Prime Process. We want to push marketing and product development out into the real world where they can directly observe the symptoms of the absence of value, and experience first hand the pains that their customers feel. We want the salespeople to communicate the issues they uncover as they conduct a diagnosis, and we want service and support staff to report the issues they find during the delivery and implementation of solutions. This ongoing diagnostic feedback loop creates a learning flow that, in turn, can be used to generate continuous improvement and breakthrough innovation.

How might this play out in the everyday world of business? Picture a financial software maker that has a 250-member salesforce calling on CFOs around the world. As the salespeople are busy diagnosing the problems that their prospects are experiencing, they are developing valuable information. If at the end of a month, they report back that 76 percent of the CFOs that they have called on are experiencing and have identified "Issue X" as their greatest concern and relay that information to marketing, how soon can a 50,000-piece mailing aimed at CFOs having trouble with "Issue X" be in the mail? And if the company's software does not already address "Issue X," how soon after the information is delivered can the programmers modify an existing product or develop a new one that does address the issue?

An Integrated Diagnostic Business Development Map

Now that we've talked about the prerequisites necessary to successfully execute a go-to-market strategy and the mechanisms that create them, we can take a high-altitude look at the way in which a go-to-market strategy is achieved. This sequence of events that forms a path from the corporate vision and value proposition to the ultimate goal of a business—the establishment of profitable, loyal, long-term customer relationships, is called the Integrated Diagnostic Business Development (IDBD) Map; its flow is illustrated in Figure 9.1.

The IDBD Map is focused on the creation of value. An organization's concept of value grows out of its vision. This vision provides the framework from which its corporate strategy evolves and a value proposition is derived. The value proposition, along with the products and services it generates, is delivered to the customer through a series of strategies that together comprise a go-to-market strategy.

The market strategy defines the marketplace in which the company will do business. It identifies the markets and market segments in which the company will sell its products and services. The competitive strategy defines a company's position with regard to other organizations within its market spaces. It identifies other companies vying for business in the same marketplaces, evaluates their strengths and weaknesses, and offers a plan to successfully compete against them. The product strategy defines the company's products and services. It determines how each will fit the particular market segment for which it is designed. Finally, sales strategy defines how the company's product and services will be offered to customers. The sales strategy is created at three levels: the customer or enterprise level, the opportunity

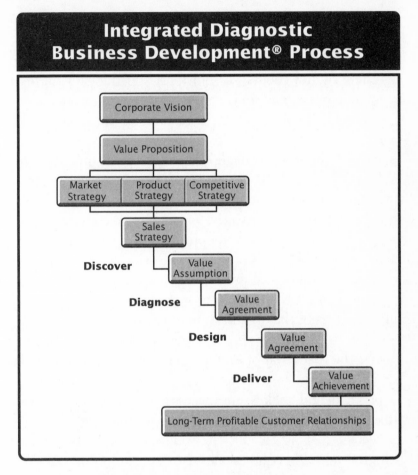

FIGURE 9.1 Integrated Diagnostic
Business Development Process®

level, and the individual or appointment level. It details the content and flow of the sales process and diagnostic strategy.

The corporate value proposition is the cornerstone that supports each of the four strategies. The purpose of those strategies is to deliver the promise of the value proposition to market and, ultimately, to individual customers. The process unfolds through the same value sequence described at the end of Chapter 3: The value proposition is extended to the market, yielding assumptions about customers' situations and the ability of the company's offerings to address those issues; the value assumption is explored, yielding agreement about the problems being experienced and their best solutions; and the value agreement is delivered and, in turn, yields value achievement.

The IDBD process is traveled twice in the creation and delivery of value. The first pass through the process occurs as each of the four strategies under the go-to-market umbrella is developed. In this way, a company can ensure that each element of its strategic plan for creating value is aligned to the needs of its prospective customers. We confirm that we can leverage value via the product, process, and performance levels of our customers organization. In other words, we want to be sure that our strategies are capable of delivering value during their planning stages before we devote the full resources of the organization to realizing them.

The second pass through the IDBD process occurs during the execution of each of the four strategies. In this pass, a company ensures that each strategy actually works as planned and makes any necessary corrections in real time. In other words, we want to ensure that each strategy succeeds—that it fulfills the value proposition we are bringing to market and creates the expected value assumption, agreement, and achievement.

When the Integrated Diagnostic Business Development Process is successfully traversed, the go-to-market strategy is realized, value is delivered to customers and value is returned to the business in the form of increased margins. The by-product of this end result is the lifeblood of corporate success—long term, profitable customer relationships. The corporate vision has been transformed into bottom-line results.

10

A Complex Sales Future

*You Can Watch It Happen to You or You
Can Make It Happen for You*

The same forces that are driving today's sales environment are shaping the structure and focus of tomorrow's sales world. We described how the forces of commoditization and complexity have changed the sales environment to the point that the assumptions on which conventional selling methodologies are based are no longer accurate reflections of today's marketplace. These two forces are clearly splitting the world of sales into two distinct groups.

This split, a chasm that will continue to widen, is in the process of creating two separate sales environments. On one side of the chasm, the typical sale will be a self-service, commodity-based, cost-driven transaction—what we call a *nonprescription* sale. On the other side, the process will be a complex, value-driven transaction—a *prescription* sale that will continue to require the guidance of an experienced team of professionals.

The sales professional's future on the commodity side of the chasm is not very secure. In 1999, it was reported that as many as half of all existing sales positions will be gone within five years.[1] That report came near the height of the Internet Revolution, and it isn't hard to understand how some experts could forecast that half the salesforce would simply disappear. After all, many experts were claiming that the entire "Old Economy" was quickly becoming obsolete. In the process, online vendors with virtual auctions and other electronic marketplaces will soon replace existing salesforces.

This hasn't happened as quickly as many predicted, but behind the overly grim statistics, there is a strong kernel of truth. Internet technology is an effective means of providing access to product information and a rapid education of customers; thus, many products and services are treated as commodities. In this scenario, customers can self-diagnose, design their solutions, and serve themselves. As a result, comparisons on price, convenience, and transaction cost become the driving force in the market. One recent example dramatically illustrates the point: In 2002, e-commerce retailer Buy.com decided to build its share of online book sales. It announced that it would beat Amazon's already discounted book prices by 10 percent. The day the price cut went into effect, Buy.com's daily book revenues increased 800 percent, and its daily average of new customers nearly tripled.[2] That's a commodity market and a *nonprescription* product.

There really isn't room for a dedicated salesforce in the nonprescription, commodity sale. In fact, sales professionals are an unnecessary and high-risk expense. When salespeople are not adding value via diagnosis, design, and delivery, their presence cannot be justified. Any loss in the number of sales jobs in coming years will come at the expense of those who are allowing their offerings to be treated as commodities. That is why we expect to see the demand for sales professionals decreasing in numbers and the remaining positions filled by highly skilled sales consultants.

On the other side of the chasm in the sales world is the complex sale. As we have shown, this sale cannot be turned into a self-service transaction. Customers do not have the knowledge or resources necessary to self-diagnose and/or design the solutions that they need as well as implement those solutions. They require the assistance and support of a professional team.

The forces of commoditization and complexity are both acting on the complex sale, but the more complex problems and solutions become, the less the sale should be transacted with simple decision making that characterizes a commodity-like transaction. Further, because of advances in technology and intense competition, the rates at which innovation and change occur are accelerating. As a result, both the problems and their solutions tend to get more difficult to understand, analyze, and evaluate. In other words, complex sales are getting even more difficult to manage, and more and more products and services that require this type of interaction are appearing in the marketplace.

For all of these reasons, we see the complex sales arena growing at a rapid rate. Today, there are roughly 16 million sales jobs in the United States. Of those, we estimate that 5 million positions are in complex environments. Because of the trend toward increasing complexity, we expect to see employment and compensation expand on that side of the chasm.

To summarize, the sales world will continue to split into two models. One is the commodity-based transaction where few salespeople will be needed. The other is the complex transaction where skilled sales professionals will be required more urgently than ever. This is why we believe that complex sales will dominate the future of the sales profession, and great compensation will be available for those who compete there. Accordingly, sales professionals who want to ensure successful careers need to seriously pursue mastery of the complex sale.

Choosing Sides

The interesting thing about the splitting of the sales world is that organizations often have a large degree of choice about whether to bring their offerings to market using either the commodity model or the complex model.

Companies can decide which side their services and products will occupy.

Some companies, especially in the business-to-business sector, do not fall cleanly into a commodity or complex transaction. They are already straddling the chasm and will be forced to either choose one selling model for their entire organization or clearly segment their markets and products into one of the two models. The one option that is not viable is to continue to allow the conventional salesforce to cover both sides of the spectrum.

Other companies are operating in markets that are already defined as either commodity markets or complex markets. But that doesn't mean that they can't change their business model and switch sides. For example, after reading about Buy.com, you might think that book selling is always a commodity transaction. Then a company such as KnowledgeMax, Inc., comes along and turns business-to-business book selling into a complex transaction. KnowledgeMax offers its organizational clients custom-designed intranets through which their employees can buy books and other educational materials. The client and its employees get the convenience of the electronic corporate bookstores and the financial efficiencies of centralized purchasing free. KnowledgeMax generates its profits the same way Buy.com does—from the orders that it fulfills.

The difference between what KnowledgeMax and Buy.com offer their customers can be expressed in terms of added value. Both companies sell books to business people, but the value in buying a book from Buy.com lies almost wholly in its discounted price. At KnowledgeMax, on the other hand, there is a great deal of created value, such as organizationwide access to targeted educational materials, the customer's ability to monitor and approve purchases, and the efficiencies involved in reducing payments for all book purchases to a single invoice. Buy.com may sell a book at a lower price, but when all of the costs of a complete transaction are calculated, the total cost of buying that book from KnowledgeMax is often substantially lower.

With the sales world splitting apart, the question you need to answer is: "Which model should my company pursue?"

There is no simple answer to this question. If your company can squeeze more cost out of the system than your competitors can, competing in the commodity sale may be a viable choice. Certainly, there are companies that have become very successful by sticking to a low cost, high volume strategy. Competing on price is, however, a two-edged sword. As soon as someone else figures out a way to beat your price, customers will switch their allegiance.

We believe that a value creation sales model ultimately offers a more profitable opportunity than a price-based sales model. It is the complex sale that offers the opportunity to create value for your customer and capture value for your organization. The complex sale allows you to differentiate your company from the rest of the field and capture and defend a competitive advantage in the marketplace. For all of these reasons, organizations that have a choice would do well to choose to embrace and develop a complex sales model.

The two key issues for those who choose the complex sale then become:

1. Can you create true measurable and incremental value for your customers and capture a share of that value for you and your organization?

2. Do you have a process that allows your customers to comprehend the absence of that value in their businesses

and be willing to pay a reasonable premium in price to receive that value?

Shaping the Future

For those who choose to pursue a high-value strategy, the final advice we offer is to move quickly to embrace the complex model to secure your future. As with most strategies, the companies that take the lead in shaping the sales environment in which they operate are more likely to succeed than those who follow the leaders.

The hard reality of the marketplace dictates that you are either part of your system or somebody else's. If you are working your system, you are in control of your destiny. If you are in the latter, odds are you will end up a victim.

This conclusion is supported by a McKinsey & Company study that examined the corporate strategies of 50 of the best-performing companies during the 10-year period between 1985 and 1995. The companies were chosen for their sales, profit, and market capitalization growth and were drawn from a variety of industries including retail, computer, manufacturing, business services, health care, and financial services. The study revealed that 86 percent of the "biggest business winners" had focused their strategies on shaping their markets.[3] In other words, a substantial majority of these highly successful companies had attempted to create their own playing fields rather than accepting and adapting to the existing market parameters.

The Diagnostic Business Development process enables you to differentiate yourself from the competition early and often and create value through the selling process itself. As we have seen, the ability to make a high-quality decision is not a common capability among customers in the complex environment. It is the value the Prime Process creates and captures that gives it the power to define our customers' expectations and shape our marketplaces.

The Prime professional brings a diagnostic, value-based decision process to the complex situation and establishes a position in the customer's mind that competitors,

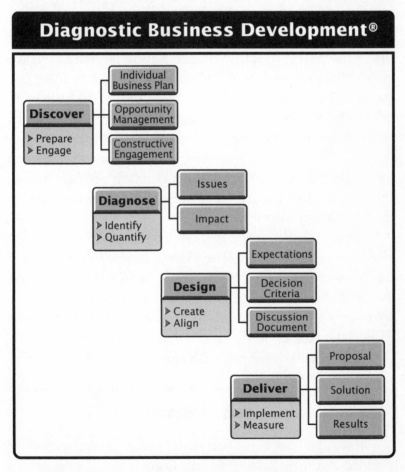

FIGURE 10.1 Diagnostic Business Development®—
The Prime Process

especially conventional salespeople, will find hard to dislodge. Think back on your own experiences with salespeople. What outcomes characterized your most positive buying experiences? For us, the best buying experiences have been those in which salespeople helped us reach high-quality decisions with all that it implies—no matter what the product or service we were purchasing.

Ultimately, there are three selling systems vying for supremacy in any particular sales engagement: the customer's system, the competitor's system, and your system. You can get caught up in the customer's system; in fact, that is the course of action that conventional selling recommends. But customer systems are usually aimed at acquiring goods and services at the lowest price and, as we have seen, rarely lead to a high-quality decision. You can fall prey to your competitors' selling system, but, of course, it is designed to stack the deck to deal them a winning hand and you will find yourself constantly reacting to their smoke and mirrors. Or, finally, you can bring your own system to the complex transaction.

The final alternative is always the best. When you provide the system, you have the highest degree of professional control over the results. When that system is the Diagnostic Business Development process, you are well on your way to *mastering the complex sale* and being able to compete and win when the stakes are high.

Allow me to leave you with one final key thought.

Key Thought

There is no Magic!—Spectacular success is always preceded by unspectacular preparation.

Whether it is Tiger Woods, Michael Jordan, Walt Disney, Roger Penske, an Olympic athlete, an accomplished musician, a respected physician, a successful business person, or it could be a top sales or service professional in your organization, whenever you watch a pro doing what they do, it may look like magic—but it's not. It is systems, it is skills, and, above all, it is discipline. The spectacular success we see is always preceded by unspectacular preparation we don't see. So enjoy your preparation and enjoy your success!

Notes

Chapter 1: The World in Which We Sell

1. Brendan Mathews, "Plane Crazy: The Joint Strike Fighter Story," *Bulletin of the Atomic Scientists* (May/June 1998).
2. Clayton M. Christensen, *The Innovator's Dilemma* (Boston: Harvard Business School Press, 1997), p. xxiii.
3. See note 2, p. xxii.

Chapter 2: Trapped in the Conventional Sales Paradigm

1. See Geoffrey A. Moore, *Crossing the Chasm: Marketing and Selling High-Tech Products to Mainstream Customers* (New York: Harper Business, 1999), for an in-depth exploration of the challenges inherent in the introduction of newly developed solutions into the marketplace at large.
2. Bill Lucas, *Power Up Your Mind: Learn Faster, Work Smarter* (Nicholas Brealey, 2001), p. 126 for retention rules of thumb.

Chapter 3: A Proven Approach to Complex Sales

1. The findings of the sales survey are recorded in, *You're Working Too Hard to Make the Sale* (Homewood, IL: Irwin, 1995), p. 16.

Chapter 4: Discover the Prime Customer

1. According to the 16th edition of *Bartlett's Familiar Quotations* (Boston: Little, Brown, 1992), the admonition to "know thyself" dates from between 650—550 B.C. It was inscribed at the Oracle of Delphi Shrine in Greece.

2. See Gerry Spence's *How to Argue and Win Every Time* (New York: St. Martin's Press, 1995), p. 134 for excellent practical advice on effective communication.

Chapter 5: Diagnose the Complex Problem

1. Dr. Sacks' quote appeared in *Forbes*, (August 21, 2000), p. 304.

2. This example is based on an actual situation in which a client of ours used a similar cost analysis to sell its equipment to a national chain of drugstores.

Chapter 7: Delivering on the Prime Promise

1. See Tom Sant's *Persuasive Business Proposals* (Amacom, 1992) for a step-by-step process to help you organize, write, and deliver successful proposals.

2. Donna Greiner and Theodore Kinni, *1,001 Ways to Keep Customers Coming Back* (Rocklin, CA: Prima, 1999), p. 148.

3. See note 1, p. 128, according to the findings of a study conducted by the *Harvard Business Review*.

Chapter 8: Prime Performance Leadership

1. Joe Gibbs with Ken Abraham, *Racing to Win: Establish Your Game Plan for Success* (Sisters, OR: Multnomah Publication, 2002), p. 267.

2. The discussion appears on pp. 9–10 of *How to Hire and Develop Your Next Top Performer* by Herb Greenberg and Harold Weinstein Patrick Sweeney (New York: McGraw-Hill, 2001).

3. The widely used DISC model was designed by Dr. William Moulton Marston in the 1920s to explain and predict how people would respond in favorable and unfavorable conditions. It measures four behavioral response styles: dominance, influence, supportiveness, and conscientiousness.

4. A proverb quoted by Aristotle circa 350 B.C., according to *Bartlett's Familiar Quotations* 16th ed. (Boston: Little, Brown, 1992), p. 78.

5. See Patricia Benner, *From Novice to Expert* (Reading, MA: Addison-Wesley, 1984).

Chapter 9: Prime Corporate Strategies

1. Smith's famous example appeared in 1776 in his book, *An Inquiry Into the Nature and Causes of the Wealth of Nations*. It illustrated how 10 workers could raise their combined output from under 200 pins per day to over 48,000 pins per day by dividing their labor so that each worker performed only one repetitive task.

2. This is also known as the Silo Effect.

3. See Peter Senge's *The Fifth Discipline: The Art and Practice of the Learning Organization* (New York: Doubleday, 1990); Peter Senge, Art Kleiner, Charlotte Roberts, Richard Ross, Bryan Smith's *The Fifth Discipline Fieldbook: Strategies and Tools for Building the Learning Organization* (New York: Doubleday, 1994) for a complete exposition of his ideas.

4. Gordon Moore is quoted from an interview conducted by Anthony Perkins, "The Accidental Entrepreneur," *Red Herring* (September 1995). Also available online at http://www.herring.com/mag/issue23/accidental.html.

Chapter 10: A Complex Sales Future

1. Neil Rackham and John DeVincentis, *Rethinking the Sales-force* (McGraw-Hill, 1999), p. 3.

2. As reported in the company's press release, "Books Sales Soar" (June 26, 2002), available at Buy.com.

3. See Hugh Courtney, "Making the Most of Uncertainty," *McKinsey Quarterly*, no. 4 (Fall, 2001).

Index